THE ILLUSTRATED HISTORY OF
BRITISH RAILWAYS

THE ILLUSTRATED HISTORY OF
BRITISH RAILWAYS

FOREWORD BY SIR PETER PARKER

CONSULTANT EDITORS
GEOFFREY FREEMAN ALLEN AND PATRICK WHITEHOUSE

ARTHUR BARKER LIMITED LONDON
A subsidiary of Weidenfeld (Publishers) Limited

Published in Great Britain by
Arthur Barker Limited
91, Clapham High Street
London SW4 7TA

Produced by Basinghall Books Limited
59, Cambridge Road
Kings Heath
Birmingham

Designed by Bob Burroughs

ISBN 213 16811 1

Printed in Hong Kong by
South China Printing Co.

jacket front:
One of Oliver Bulleid's
West Country class light
Pacifics runs out her days on
the Waterloo–Bournemouth–
Weymouth trains in 1967.
(Derek Cross)

jacket back:
An East Coast main line HST
on the Kings Cross–
Edinburgh run in 1980.
(PM Robinson)

CONTENTS

FOREWORD
BY SIR PETER PARKER

It is good to be so vividly reminded of our amazing history, and good to sense the individual effort which was at the heart of it all. This effort is still there, even in the gloom of recession, to see the way to a brighter future at the end of the century. Then over 50% should be electrified and a Channel tunnel will link the island railway to Western Europe and beyond.

This book follows the saga from the early days. It is a magnificent pictorial record of the origins, of Railway Mania, of the Golden Years, through war and peace and war again to nationalization and the end of the steam era. And then it goes through to the High Speed age in which, with all the problems of sustaining investment, we give the community a service which is unique in frequency, speed and comfort.

We have problems, of course, and share difficult economic conditions with the rest of the country. But, both in freight and passenger transit, we can win through, adapting, modernising and making the railways an efficient and profitable transport medium for an advanced industrial community.

This History makes me feel aware of the force and drive of the pride that there is in the service of railways. It has come through many radical changes, but it is a sound basis for confidence in the railways in the future.

Seeing the past, set fascinatingly, magnificently in this book, I see the future with a matching exhilaration.

8

1

THE FIRST RAILWAYS

BIRTH OF THE STEAM RAILWAY

Although the public railway has been with us for over 150 years kinds of railways go far back into history: their origin in a form of guidance system for carts and wagons is lost in the mists of time. Perhaps the earliest record dates back to Roman days when it was known for ruts to be dug in mountain roads to prevent wheeled vehicles from straying too close to the edge of a precipice. But it was really the mines of mediaeval central Europe which can claim to be the pioneers of railways. By the fifteenth century timber baulks were being laid to provide a smooth route over rough ground for ease of movement: this system was gradually improved to include a vertical guide pin attached to the underside of the vehicle so that it protruded into a slot between the planks; this prevented the barrows from slipping off the edges. The logical extension to this practice, especially where heavy horse drawn vehicles were concerned was to use a raised timber edge rail which adequately prevented the wheels from leaving the running surface. It took a long time for the final step where the flanged wheel replaced the flanged rail.

In Britain coal mining was an established industry by the early eighteenth century, especially in the north east where the coalfields were reasonably close to navigable rivers and the sea, for example Tyneside. Arising from this it was sensible that wagonways should be built from the pithead to the Tyne allowing the coal to be carried onward by the cheapest carrier of all – the ship. The L-section cast iron plate rail had been invented for mine use by John Curr in 1787 and this not only revolutionised the transport of coal underground but it also quickly lead to the adoption of mineral wagonways on the surface. The next step was the use of the iron wheel in place of the wooden cartwheel thus providing freer running and a greater hauling capacity for each horse – no longer was an animal necessarily limited to one vehicle. It took a little time for the next simple invention – the replacement of the flanged rail by the flanged wheel but once this tremendous advantage was realised then it superseded all other designs for the transportation of rolling stock over iron rails. And so it is today – the standard railway principle throughout the world.

Steam too was first used industrially in connection with mining

Early sketches of Mining Railways in Central Europe circa 16th Century. (Colourviews Picture Library)

right:
Early plateway track, Little Eaton. Note stone sleepers. (Colourviews Picture Library)

projects; its prime purpose was to power vast and cumbersome pumps in an attempt to deal with the ever present problem of water seepage. As we have seen earlier coal mining was well established in north east England by the beginning of the nineteenth century but the Cornish tin mines had also been an important part of the mining scene for many centuries. In both these areas early and crude steam powered engines had been used for nearly a century to work the pumps which extracted the water from deep workings. In those days, however, there was little practical knowledge of the application of materials and design techniques to take advantage of the capabilities which steam power could

offer. The first successful machine was the famous Newcomen engine built to pump water near Dudley Castle in Worcestershire as far back as 1712. This and all the earlier engines did not use steam as a direct method of propulsion but to create a vacuum against which atmospheric pressure reacted to move a piston. The volume of steam required to create this vacuum meant that the Newcomen engines were huge, clumsy and slow running and it was not until James Watt improved the position by enclosing both ends of the cylinder, making the piston double acting, that matters improved considerably. The final step came when the Cornishman Richard Trevithick so designed an engine

right:
Belvoir Castle Railway wagon. (Colourviews Picture Library)

A Peak Forest Tramway wagon used for carrying limestone. Note flangeless wheels on plateway track. (Colourviews Picture Library)

where the pressure of steam was directly responsible for moving the piston, at the same time allowing the exhaust to discharge into the atmosphere rather than to condense. This was a great advance for the harnessing of steam at high pressure enabled more power to be generated from a cylinder of given size. Trevithick made the reciprocating steam engine, as it is known today, a possibility.

But it was not quite as simple as that for the pioneers were entering an area completely unknown and to some unnatural. By 1801 Trevithick had constructed a road engine and in 1803 he was closely involved in the design and construction of what is today accepted as the first steam locomotive to run on rails: this was at Coalbrookdale ironworks in Shropshire. The following year his second working steam locomotive hauled a ten-ton load over a distance of 9.5 miles in four hours on the Pen-y-Darren Tramway in South Wales: the trial won a wager of 500 guineas! But this trial presaged a problem which was to haunt many a locomotive builder in the years to come: the weight of the engine was too much for the track and the rails fractured.

left:
Although this print shows the two engines used to haul trains from Euston to Camden Town on the London & Birmingham Railway, their purpose, to move the steel ropes, was not new in the 1830s.

below:
Richard Trevithick's pioneer engine of 1803. (Colourviews Picture Library)

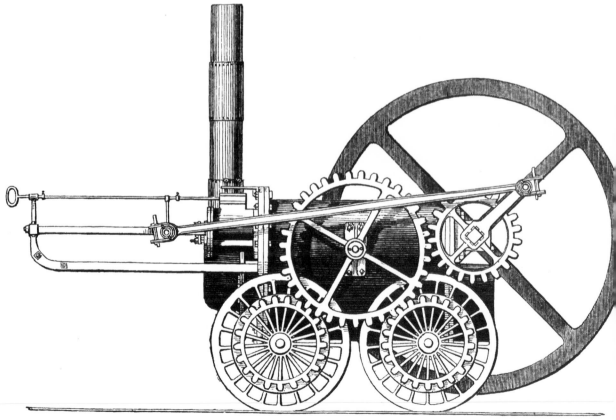

An early road steam coach of the turn of the 18th century This colour print portrays Goldsworthy Gurney's vehicle weighing some 2 tons with an intended travelling rate of 8–10 miles per hour.

16

Consequently it only had a short life as a locomotive before it took up its originally intended function – driving a steam hammer in the ironworks. Sadly none of Trevithick's four locomotives including one built for Blackett of Wylam near Newcastle was put to prolonged commercial use: his final engine of 1808 hauled passenger wagons round a circular track as an entertainment near now what is the University of London at Euston. It was nicknamed the *Catch Me Who Can*. This was, all in all, an inauspicious start to the use of a steam engine on rails.

So the designer of the steam locomotive was faced with a dilemma – his difficulty was that not only had he to produce a locomotive which was not too heavy to damage the track but also one which *was* heavy enough to provide the necessary grip between the wheels and the iron rails to prevent slipping; to make matters worse a number of the horse drawn tramroads and railways had been built with severe gradients which made adhesion even more difficult. The reason for this form of construction was that the horse could pull the empty wagons up the hill and the loaded train, horse included, could run down by gravity. It took some time before this challenge was overcome and the first success story (in 1812) was that of the Middleton Railway near Leeds where the inventiveness of John Blenkinsop produced a combination of a rack with running rails.

The following year William Hedley showed, by means of some very cleverly designed experiments, that it was possible to obtain enough adhesion for the transmission of power via the locomotive's wheels. In that momentous year of 1813 his *Puffing Billy* and *Wylam Dilly* engines entered service, but even they were too heavy for the early iron track and had to be rebuilt with eight carrying wheels instead of four: later – when technology had improved and track strengthened they reverted to four wheelers. *Puffing Billy* was the first locomotive with more than one axle powered – this was achieved by gearing: the engine is now exhibited in the Science Museum at South Kensington. *Wylam Dilly* too has been saved for posterity and resides in the Royal Scottish Museum in Edinburgh.

This progress was carefully noticed by George Stephenson who was employed as an assistant fireman at one of the collieries. By the time he was in his early thirties Stephenson had become enginewright for a group of collieries around Killingworth and he became fascinated by the idea of overcoming some of the inherent problems of the operation of steam engines. He was able to develop his own plans and at the same time worked out his principles of railway construction and operation: these before long were to find widespread and indeed universal application.

Stephenson faced many design problems with the early locomotives for a great deal of progress had to be achieved by trial and error. He was able to simplify certain elements of the Trevithick design, for example, cylinders were sited at one end of the boiler thus simplifying the transmission of thrust to the driving wheels. Cross-beams on the

left:
A painting by J. E. Wigston of Stephenson's *Locomotion*.

below:
A page from Rastrick's notebook of 1829 preserved in the Goldsmith Company's Economic Library, University of London. The *Experiment* was supplied by Robert Stephenson & Co. to the Stockton & Darlington Railway in 1828.
(Colourviews Picture Library)

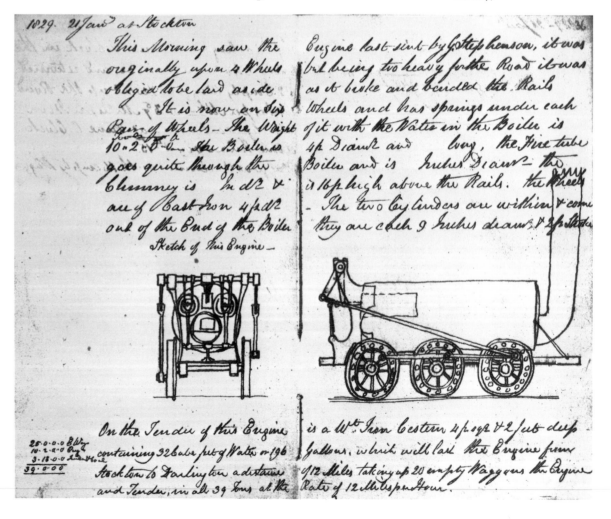

THE "SANSPAREIL" OF MR HACKWORTH OF DARLINGTON,

WHICH DRAWING A LOAD EQUIVALENT TO THREE TIMES ITS WEIGHT TRAVELLED AT THE RATE OF 12½ MILES AN HOUR, COST FOR FUEL PER MILE ABOUT TWO PENCE.

The replica *Rocket* built in 1979 by Locomotion Enterprises on a demonstration track in Hyde Park, London. (British Rail)

Liverpool & Manchester Railway. A scene in Olive Mount Cutting – from an Ackerman print. (British Rail/OPC)

left:
Replicas of *Northumbrian* and *Rocket* stood in Derby locomotive works during the 1930s. (P B Whitehouse Collection)

tops of the long piston rods confined the thrusts during each revolution of the wheels to a comparatively small amount and this helped the primitive slide bars or parallel motion arrangements to withstand the force. He also looked at the vital problem of shock and introduced a primitive form of springing – a great help when one considers the dreadful irregularities in the rough permanent way of the period: it ensured also that maximum adhesion was obtained. As a converse the springing also reduced the shock load to the rails and this at least cut down the number of rail breakages.

It was not long before Stephenson's reputation spread whilst at the same time it was also becoming apparent that railways and steam locomotives offered advantages for collieries away from navigable waterways. Inflation was rife, for example the price of horse fodder had soared as a result of the Napoleonic Wars and with these factors in mind Stephenson's employers instructed him to build a locomotive for their Killingworth Railway; his first machine *Blucher* took to the rails in 1814. Between that year and 1826, lean years for business, Stephenson was the only man in Britain to build locomotives; through his association with the ironmasters William Losh and Michael Longridge he was responsible for the further development of cast iron rails and wheels as well as the first steel springs to carry weights of several tons. By the mid 1820's the results were beginning to look promising and there began to be talk of the building of steam operated railways: the first was the Stockton and Darlington where George Stephenson was appointed engineer in 1821. What made this railway unique was the fact that its main line from Shildon to Darlington – a distance of 22 miles – was laid out for locomotive haulage. Not only was this the longest locomotive hauled route to use locomotives but it was also the first railway to use them to handle public traffic. It opened in 1825.

The next, and in many ways the most momentous project, was the Liverpool and Manchester Railway. It was 30 miles long and Stephenson was appointed engineer: work began in 1826. But while the Stockton and Darlington was basically a colliery railway whose *raison d'etre* was the transport of coal from mine to wharf, the Liverpool and Manchester was the world's first line to provide the principal link for all classes of traffic between two large cities. Investors had seen that the time was ripe to set up a new transport system in Britain.

It was hardly surprising that this venture met with opposition in view of the strength of the waterway systems in Lancashire – indeed waterborne carriage rates were cut by 25% in advance of the railway's opening to dissuade potential customers from switching their allegiance. But in 1824, even before his Stockton and Darlington project had been completed Stephenson's survey of the Liverpool and Manchester route had been completed and the requisite Bill presented before Parliament. It was a further year, after a fuller survey, before the opposition was bought off and the Act passed.

This was the beginning of the great railway age: thousands of labourers were brought in to remove all obstacles and to construct the line and today the labour intensiveness of it all would make any promoter blanch. But it must be remembered that civil engineering as such was in its absolute infancy and one can only admire the work of those pioneer engineers and contractors. Some of the work on this first inter-city line was breathtaking in its size and daring. A cutting 70ft deep, Olive Mount, on the outskirts of Liverpool, was hewn out of solid rock; a superb viaduct of nine arches carried the double track over the Sankey Valley and the rails were laid over the troublesome and uneasy surface of Chat Mass.

But a new railway of this kind obviously needed new and improved motive power and during 1829 the directors of the L&M advertised that they would give a prize to the builder of the locomotive which had met their requirements at a contest to be held that autumn on a completed section of the line at Rainhill. The conditions were onerous. The engine should not weigh more than $4\frac{1}{2}$ tons (if four wheeled) or 6 tons (if six wheeled) excluding tender; it should use steam at no more than 50lb per square inch, but the boiler must be tested hydraulically to three times that figure; it had to 'consume its own smoke' because an Act of Parliament said so; and it had to haul a load of three times its own weight for a total of 75 miles at 10mph. This was not a race and competitors had to observe stringent regulations; each locomotive had to travel 37.5 miles twice – representing the return trip between Liverpool and Manchester. However, the distance was not covered in two straight journeys but by the locomotive travelling backwards and forwards over the 1.75 mile course. On the first day some 15,000 sightseers watched the trials.

Stephenson entered his new *Rocket* an engine which was a considerable improvement over his *Locomotion* for the Stockton and Darlington and, as it proved, over the other competitors *Sansparail* and *Novelty* built by Timothy Hackworth and Braithwaite & Ericsson respectively. The locomotive had an entirely new design of boiler using many small tubes to convey the heat to the water instead of a single large one, the cylinders were removed from their vertical position and placed at an inclination and for the first time weight and expense were saved by using only one pair of driving wheels. The *Rocket* was simpler and

more robust than its predecessors and therefore more efficient; it romped away with the £500 prize. *Rocket* was the first locomotive to incorporate, albeit in fairly simple form, the principal features necessary to propel a machine by steam successfully and economically. As with so many pioneering machines, it was soon to be overtaken by events and proved too small for the huge traffic generated by its owning railway.

The Liverpool and Manchester Railway opened on 15th September 1830. Eight special trains conveyed both dignitaries and also the common people from Liverpool to Manchester; the guest of honour was the then Prime Minister, the Duke of Wellington. Sadly it was his train which was involved in the first fatality involving a passenger train; as it stood at Parkside for the locomotive to take on water William Huskisson, MP for Liverpool and President of the Board of Trade, left the Prime Minister's carriage and was crushed between the side of it and *Rocket* which was hauling a train on the adjacent track. That night, in Eccles, he became the first man to die from injuries arising from a railway accident.

The success of the Liverpool and Manchester Railway was immediate and it is said that within three months over half the stage coaches which plied between the two cities were off the road. By the end of 1830 the railway was able to report a net profit of £14,432 on just three and a half month's operation. The age of the passenger carrying steam railway had arrived.

THE NETWORK EMERGES

Within five years of the opening of the Stockton & Darlington Railway the role of the railway in Britain was changing. Instead of being regarded merely as a short-haul transport system primarily of benefit to industry, it was seen as the primary means of moving people as well as freight between major cities.

While many powerful individuals and lobbies remained against the railways and fought hard to keep the builders away, others were equally determined that any proposed line should be built in such a way as to serve all the major towns near the projected route. More often than not their proposals were not only uneconomic but also doomed to failure because of topographical problems. The construction, for example, of a railway over the 112 miles from London to Birmingham was a far more complicated and costly operation than building 31 miles of line from Liverpool to Manchester.

The London & Birmingham Railways, opened in 1837–38, was the first trunk main line from London. Its construction presented new civil engineering problems involving deep cuttings, inclines and tunnels. The line had to climb the Chiltern hills and the Northamptonshire hills and cross the rivers Avon, Ouse and Thames. George Stephenson's son, Robert, who was to be regarded by many as the greatest engineer of the era, was appointed chief engineer. He plotted the route to include gentle curves and easy gradients which involved major engineering and construction works such as the Watford and Kilsby tunnels, the deep cuttings at Tring and Roade and the long viaduct at Wolverton. Fortunately, Robert Stephenson had not only been given an excellent formal education – which his father could afford thanks to his own success – but had also gained valuable practical experience of railway building by working with George on the Stockton & Darlington and later in North America. He was perhaps the most influential of all railway engineers and his Britannia Tubular Bridge over the Menai Strait – one of the two great bridges he designed – has been described as the greatest and boldest civil engineering feat of the early Victorian era. (Two of his later bridges, at Newcastle and Berwick, completed a direct Anglo-Scottish east coast route by 1850.)

The first public passenger
railway – a scene on the
Liverpool & Manchester
Railway, drawn by
Ackerman, shows a train on
the Sankey Viaduct.
(National Railway Museum)

The southern terminus of the London & Birmingham was Euston station, which was able to claim that it was the gateway to the north because from there it was possible to reach both Liverpool and Manchester via Birmingham. This came about because the L & B's northern terminus, Curzon Street, in Birmingham, was shared with the Grand Junction Railway which linked Birmingham with those two northern cities. With the completion during the next decade of lines from Birmingham to Derby, York and beyond, Euston was the only station in the capital to serve the north. It retained this distinction until 1850, when Maiden Lane, just north of today's Kings Cross, was opened in London with the new main line to Peterborough, Doncaster and York.

Not unnaturally the ports of the south of England attracted the attention of railway builders since there was an obvious demand to link them with London. The London & Southampton was opened in stages beginning in 1837 but Southampton was then far from being the great port it is today. In fact, it was the coming of the railway and the development of steamships which encouraged Southampton to expand.

Of far greater commercial importance at the time was the city of Bristol, which was still regarded as England's second city in the early 1820s and had a thriving port. The building of the Great Western Railway from Bristol to London was therefore of major significance and the line lived up to expectations. It was superbly planned and executed, with curves and gradients reduced to the minimum by Isambard Kingdom Brunel. It was he, also, who selected the unique gauge for the GWR of 7ft 0¼in, firmly believing that this was the ideal, though it was to present problems later. From the first, though, it set the GWR apart from other companies as doing things differently.

The gauge of the Stockton & Darlington was 4ft 8in. It would be nice to accept the folklore which says that Stephenson chose this after surveying the axle widths of road carts; in fact the gauge was already in use on the wagonways of the north-east. Stephenson saw no reason to change the gauge on which he had carried out some of his early experiments when it was laid on the Killingworth lines. He had used the same gauge on the Hetton Colliery Railway and did so again on the Liverpool & Manchester. It was, of course, to become the standard gauge, though the extra half-inch (to 4ft 8½in) was allowed later to give better clearance between the reverse of the wheel flanges and the check rails. (Today standard gauge is 4ft 8⅜in, the small adjustment having been made to reduce the tendency of

The famous Doric-arch entrance to old Euston station was demolished in the 1960s to make way for the new terminus. (National Railway Museum)

left:
Excavation work for the building of the London & Birmingham Railway at Park Village, Camden, 26 August 1836. Sketch by J C Bourne. (National Railway Museum)

right:
The cutting at Mornington Crescent, 1836, a sketch by J C Bourne of the building of the London & Birmingham Railway. (National Railway Museum)

bogies to 'hunt' or vibrate laterally at high speeds.)

It was Brunel who introduced the continuous beam timber sleepers for his broad-gauge track. Previously, the iron rails had been laid separately on wooden or stone blocks in parallel rows, with stone blocks supporting the ends of each length of rail. While there were advantages to Brunel's 'baulk road' – the beams gave continuous support and held the track more accurately to its gauge – it also provided a very rough ride since it reduced the vertical give of the rail at a time when there was only a minimum of springing in rolling stock. Despite this, Brunel persisted with the continuous beam until the end of broad gauge, even though other companies had adopted the transverse beam system still followed today. Indeed the greatest advantage of Brunel's 'baulk road' was in the ease with which it could be removed when the GWR finally completed its changeover to standard gauge in May 1892 by converting the track west of Exeter in just two days!

Apart from other considerations, the broad gauge created problems because it was incompatible with standard gauge. This meant that when the lines of the GWR met those of other companies there could be no easy sharing arrangement as occurred elsewhere. Such was the extent of concern over the 'battle of the gauges' as it has become known, that Parliament set up a Gauge Commission to investigate each system. When the Commissioners visited Gloucester to witness the transfer of Bristol and Gloucester Railway freight from one system to the other they saw a scene of total chaos and delay. On the other hand, though totally unimpressed with the transfer arrangements, the Commission did come down in favour of the performance of broad-gauge locomotives over those of narrow-gauge. However, that was not enough to stop them from recommending that in future all railways should be built to the standard gauge. Opposition by the GWR to the Gauge Bill made it less restrictive than it might have been and even after it became law, railway companies were able to specify exemption from standard gauge. Broad gauge could still be used for lines built in areas already covered by the GWR. The peak of broad gauge was in the mid-1860s, when 1040 miles of broad and 387 miles of mixed gauge had been laid from London to Weymouth, Penzance, New Milford and Wolverhampton. Even so, inroads had been made by standard gauge into this territory, whose borders were

right:
Side elevation from the general arrangement drawing of the Great Western Railway 7' 0" gauge *North Star* as reconstructed at Swindon in 1925.
(P B Whitehouse Collection)

TABLE OF FARES

FROM LONDON TO BIRMINGHAM AND LIVERPOOL,

AND FROM STATION TO STATION.

N.B.—*The fares by the Night Trains are something more than those enumerated below.*

Grand Junction Railway table of fares soon after the opening in 1837, first and second class only. (P B Whitehouse collection)

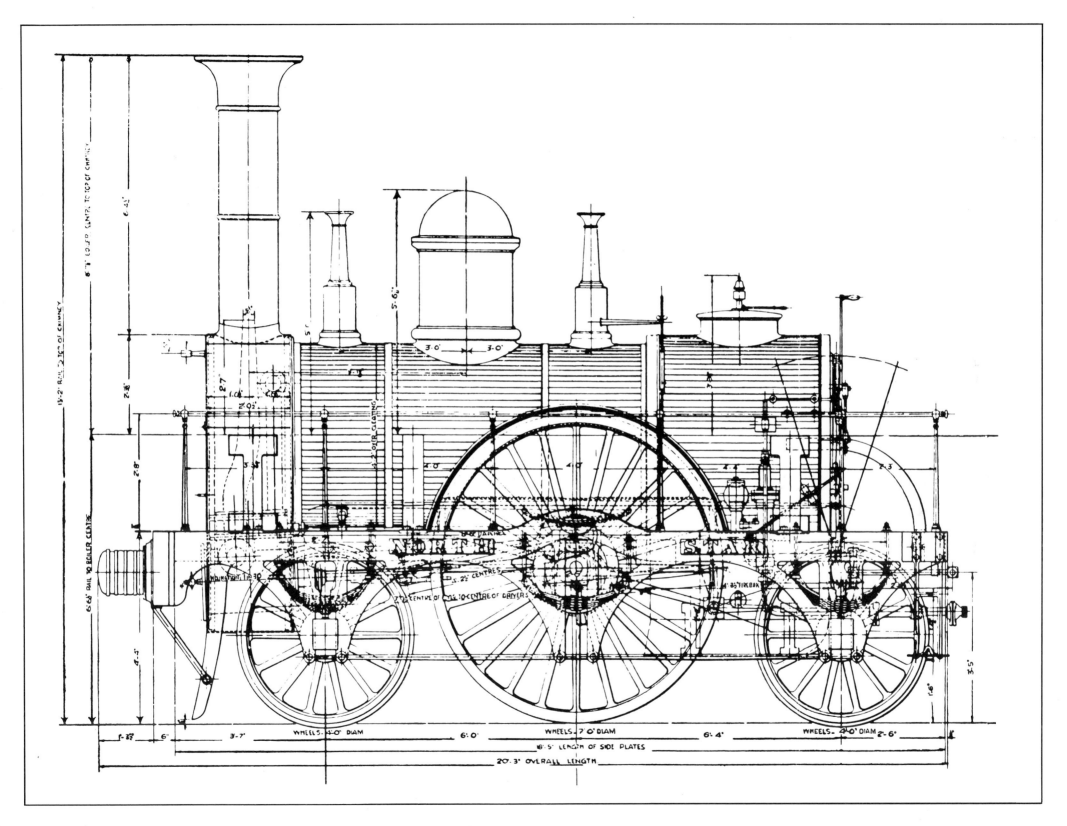

also surrounded by 4ft 8½in tracks.

Brunel was nothing if not an innovator and he adopted an unusual method of propulsion for the South Devon Railway's extensions through the county – the use of the atmospheric system. Though the line was, like other continuations of the broad-gauge system, built by a separate company, the GWR had a considerable financial interest in it, as a major shareholder and as part-owner of the Bristol and Exeter Railway. Brunel was also its engineer.

Atmospheric or pneumatic propulsion had been patented by Clegg and Samuda in 1839 and had been used on the Dublin and Kingstown Railway and between Croydon and Forest Hill. The system proposed for South Devon, where it was thought that it would give easier working over the steep gradients around Dartmoor and would cut costs, involved the installation of a 15in diameter pipe between the track. A piston was attached to the leading vehicle through a slot in the top of the pipe, the slot being closed in front of the piston attachment by means of a continuous flexible flap over which a small wheel ran to make a seal behind the piston. It was then possible to exhaust the air from the pipe ahead of the piston by means of stationary pumping engines. Atmospheric pressure entered the pipe behind the piston and forced it through the tube; the train thus was pushed along.

After initial trials in the spring of 1847, the system came into public use between Exeter and Teignmouth in September. Though there were occasional mishaps and delays, the system won universal support and gave a smooth ride and a clean journey. However, complications soon arose, particularly with the leather seal. Not only did it prove to be a popular meal for wayside rats, the leather was porous and was almost permanently saturated or, in winter, frozen stiff. In addition, corrosion set in between the tannin and the fastenings. Less than a year after its public inception, the atmospheric pressure system was useless, the whole of the leather valve from Exeter to Newton Abbot having disintegrated. Faced with repairs which would cost £250,000 and the knowledge that operating costs were higher than had been estimated, the company ceased to use this method of propulsion. The subsequent sale of plant raised a mere £43,000 – a tenth of the capital cost.

Undoubtedly George Stephenson, who had dismissed the method as 'a great humbug', gained some degree of satisfaction from its failure. Nevertheless, Brunel's purpose in decreeing its adoption had been to try a new form of propulsion which could have saved some of the great cost of earthworks and tunnelling involved in trunk-route

AYLESBURY RAILWAY.

FIVE POUNDS REWARD.

Some evil-disposed Person or Persons have lately *feloniously Stolen and carried away,* a quantity of RAILS, STAKES, and MATERIALS, belonging to the Company, for which any Offender, on Conviction, is liable to Transportation for Seven Years.

Several STAKES driven into the Ground for the purpose of setting out the Line of Railway, have also been *Pulled up and Removed,* by which a Penalty of Five Pounds for each Offence has been incurred, half Payable to the Informer and half to the Company.

The above Reward will be paid on Conviction, in addition to the Penalty, to any Person who will give Evidence sufficient to Convict any Offender guilty of either of the above Crimes, on application to Mr. HATTEN or Mr. ACTON TINDAL, of Aylesbury.

By Order of the Directors.
Aylesbury, August 18th, 1838.   May, Printer, Aylesbury.

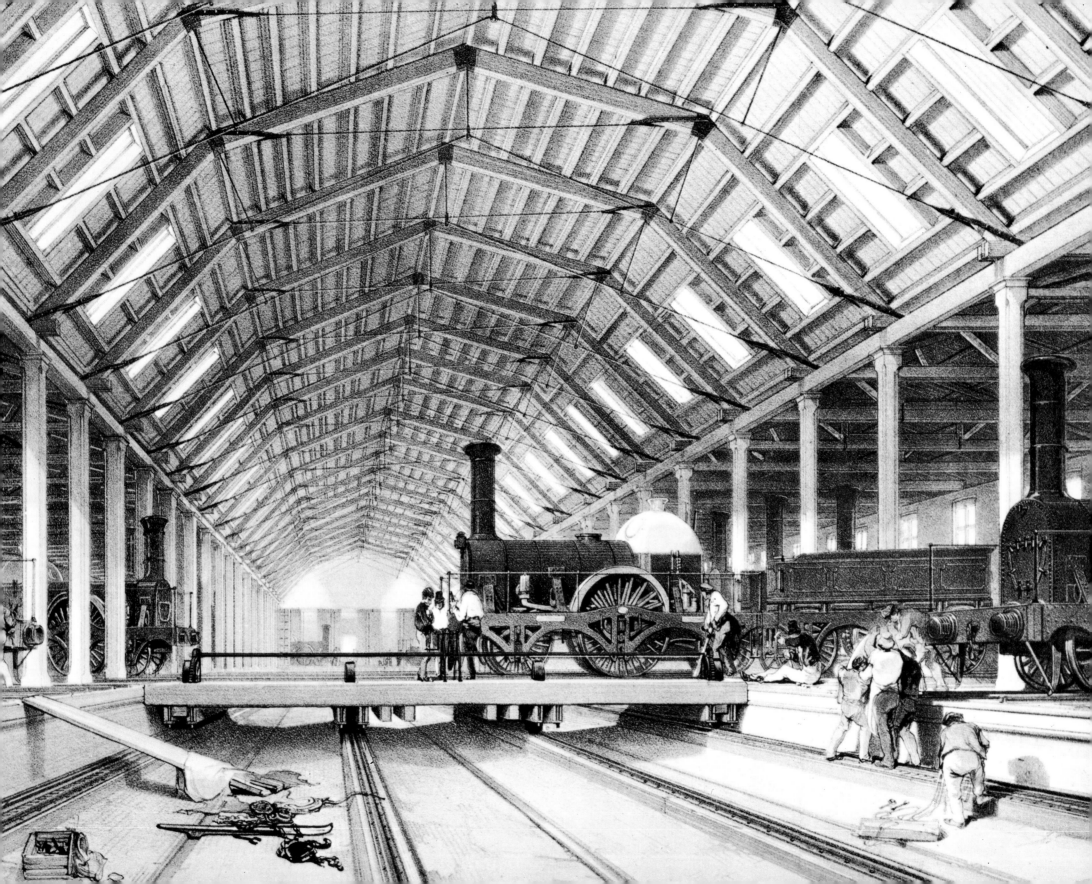

construction. The fact that the system passed its initial trials was sufficient justification for Brunel to go ahead; the presence of some excessively steep gradients in South Devon are a permanent reminder that in the end he was proved wrong.

Among those who sprang to fame as a result of the new railway age was Thomas Brassey, perhaps the pre-eminent railway contractor, who undertook the building of 1700 route miles in Britain (plus 2800 miles abroad). When Joseph Locke was working on the construction of the London and Southampton Railway, Brassey secured contracts worth £4.3 million to build 118 miles of the line. While working on the Grand Junction Railway, Locke, incidentally, had devised a system of estimating that worked well where a small force of contractors was involved. Brassey's labour force went beyond the 'small' and at one time numbered 45,000 men working in Britain and on the continent. Indeed, British railway builders spread their influence and their labour forces wide: Brassey engineered lines from Paris to Rouen, Le Havre, Nantes and Cherbourg and in Holland and Spain; Brunel surveyed lines between Florence and Pistoia and from Genoa to Alessandria in Italy; Robert Stephenson worked in Belgium, Sweden and Switzerland.

The conditions under which the workmen lived and worked on the new lines were often appalling. Shanty towns were built in the depth of the countryside while, if construction work was being carried out near towns, only the meanest of hovels and most primitive sanitary facilities were provided. The result was that death, disease and injury were commonplace. Opposite York station a burial ground was opened in 1832 for the victims of a cholera epidemic. In the six years required to build the line over the Pennine range more than 100 bodies were taken for burial at Chapel-le-Dale and others were interred near the mouth of Blea Moor Tunnel. Workmen were killed or maimed not only in major disasters such as tunnels collapsing or flooding but also in relatively simple operations. To survive, the men had to be tough and fearless and accidents often occurred when they were showing off their prowess or after drinking orgies which followed fortnightly pay-days. The men were, incidentally, known as 'navvies', a name derived from the 'navigators' who laboured to build Britain's navigable waterways a century before.

Though by no means causing death or disease, the conditions under which second- and third-class passengers travelled were also extremely primitive. They rode in open wagons, some with seats and some without, and had to suffer the smoke and cinders as well as

the extremes of the British climate. By contrast, first-class travel was luxurious: passengers rode in covered coaches with a degree of furnishing and upholstery and even oil or candle lights in some coaches. The compartments in a coach derived from the builders' intention to make the carriages as much like a terrace of stage-coaches as possible.

In fact it was possible for road travellers to take to the railways without changing carriages: the road carriages were loaded on to flat railway wagons. This was a sensible marketing idea which proved an added attraction in drawing passengers away from conventional means of road travel. The greatest advantage which the railways had, however, was that they were able to convey passengers more quickly to their destinations.

In 1835 coaching was at its peak with 3300 stage-coaches and 700 mail coaches on the roads each day. However, the Post Office had begun using the railways to transport mail on the Liverpool & Manchester as early as 1830. The introduction of stamps and the penny post by Rowland Hill in 1840 saw the railways poised to carry the flood of mail which was to follow.

When the seal of royal approval was set upon the new form of passenger transport, travel by rail became more than a convenience; it was the correct 'modern' thing to do. In 1839 Prince Albert, who was returning from a visit to Queen Victoria at Windsor, travelled on the GWR from Slough to Paddington. It was three years before the Queen herself was persuaded to journey by rail from Windsor to London but in 1840 Queen Adelaide, widow of William IV, became the first queen to use this mode of transport.

By 1842 far more passengers were using the railways than the stage-coaches. In addition, with a network of nearly 2000 miles of tracks, the railway companies were generating new freight traffic as well as continuing to attract custom away from the waterways. The framework of the main rail trunk system was laid and in operation, the people had taken to steam locomotion for themselves and their goods, and the companies were profitable with an annual revenue of about £4 million.

The curtain was about to be raised on the most dramatic period of railway construction and speculation which would see the trunk send out branches to cover the length and breadth of the country.

The Stockton and Darlington Railway Company's authorised capital when the act allowing its construction was passed in 1821 was just over £100,000 for a route of almost 27 miles, or rather less than £4000 a mile. That act had been the twenty-first passed in

Britain since the start of the century to authorise a railway to be built. By the mid-1840s Parliament was coping with a rush of such bills seeking enactment and the cost of railway construction had risen dramatically.

Total authorised capital for the whole country aggregated about £76 million for a route mileage of just over 4000 – or about £19,000 a mile. (In fact by the beginning of 1845 only 2150 miles of line had been opened to traffic.) Yet the tidal wave of new construction against which these figures become mere droplets was still to come. By the spring of the following year there were no less than 519 railway bills awaiting Parliamentary approval, involving a total share capital of around £230 million.

The railway mania had, of course, been set off by the success of some, if not all of the early companies and by the fact that there were still many areas of the country ripe for railway development. The attraction was not generally altruistic; it lay in the chance for personal prestige and fortune for those who could launch successful companies and actually see their railway operating.

Virtually every railway scheme had to have Parliamentary approval and there were various standing orders which had to be observed in an attempt to exclude all but *bona fide* applicants. Because of the queue of bills awaiting approval, attempts were made to shorten the procedure in the House of Commons but even so the presentation of each bill gave its opponents a chance to raise all kinds of objections to its contents or the likely consequences if it was passed. In particular, there was opposition from those speaking on behalf of existing railway companies which felt their own interests might be damaged by a new company in opposition.

Even after the Acts had been passed the opposition to new lines did not always stop. Apart from deliberate attempts to prevent the new companies raising the necessary capital, there were also ways of delaying the construction work itself once it got under way. Fights between navvies and gangs of 'roughs' raised by the opposition occurred quite often.

In the 1840s company accountancy was a generally haphazard affair and the companies were required only to account to their shareholders – and even then in broad detail. There was no obligation to present detailed financial accounts to Parliament, the Board of Trade or the public. It was easy enough, anyway, to conceal details of, for example, expenditure from the revenue account by lumping it under the heading of 'capital', thereby apparently increasing the profitability of an operation and, where possible, enabling dividends

to be paid out of capital. Railway companies could conceal their shaky foundations well enough to be able to continue attracting shareholders' support and new investment.

Nor was it difficult to rig the stock-market value of shares in the railway companies by forcing prices up or down artificially through bulk buying or selling of shares. There was nothing to prevent dubious characters from floating a new railway company and selling shares in it without any intention of proceeding with the flamboyant plans which had been used to attract buyers' attention. The company could simply be allowed to die or be traded off after the dubious entrepreneurs had creamed off their share of the 'profits', the investors being left with nothing. Today it seems extraordinary that in 1836 four different schemes were put before Parliament for companies to operate between London and Brighton; all were unsuccessful yet in the next Parliamentary session six more schemes were promoted.

An indication of the way in which the 'railway-rush' of the 1840s developed comes from the fact that in 1843 24 Acts were passed to permit new lines to be built; in the successive three Parliamentary sessions thereafter the number of bills presented rose to 37, then 248 and finally to 815. Over 700 of these reached the Private Bills Office, the others failing to be considered for a variety of reasons.

An *Illustrated London News* drawing of 1854 showing an impression of the new Grand Central Railway station at New Street, Birmingham. The Queens Hotel is on the right of the picture. (Colourviews Picture Library)

From 1845 to 1847 Parliament sanctioned 8592 route miles in three sessions, yet little more than one-third of that total was actually built; the balance of about 5500 miles was either abandoned or quietly forgotten.

Fortunately, despite the highly suspect nature of many of the railway companies of this period, there were those who saw to it that reputable railway construction continued. Once London was linked with north-west England, the next natural objective became Scotland. The Wigan branch of the Liverpool & Manchester had been opened in 1832 as a small step further north and in 1838 the Northern Union Railway went beyond Wigan to Preston. Two years later came the opening of the Lancaster & Preston Railway. From Lancaster the road mail coaches for Carlisle, Edinburgh and Glasgow were now timed to connect with the trains. In August of 1840, two months after this development, the Glasgow & South Western Railway opened its first section, which connected the city with Ardrossan. Previously the day mail trains between London and Liverpool had connected with the Liverpool-Ardrossan steamer; now the mail could go all the way by rail.

That year saw other important route developments. Through

trains were introduced from London Euston to York, following the London & Birmingham Railway's line to Rugby and then taking the Midland Counties Railway route through Leicester to Derby. From there the route was over North Midland tracks to Altofts Junction. The northward advance was furthered by the opening of the Preston and Wyre Railway's line to the port of Fleetwood, from where the Ardrossan steamer service operated thereafter.

The important step, though, was from Lancaster, over the West-morland fells to Carlisle. George Stephenson was not entirely happy about a route he had supported across Morecambe Bay from Hest

Bank to Kents Bank on an embankment and thence to Ulverston, Millom and Whitehaven. Joseph Locke carried out independent surveys and selected a route almost due north from Lancaster over the 915ft high Shap Fells, preferring to climb the heights rather than tunnel on grounds of cost. The challenge of this long haul was one which was important not only to civil engineers building the line but also to those who had to design the locomotives to traverse it. Today's electrically powered trains from the south barely slacken pace up the last 1-in-75, four-mile climb and even have to reduce power to remain within the 75mph speed limit but to the steam

The Chepstow tubular suspension bridge and the junction of the Severn and the Wye Rivers, 1852. From *The Illustrated London News.* (Colourviews Picture Library)

locomotives of the 1840s the climb was a trudge. The line from Lancaster to Oxenholme, near Kendal, was opened in September 1846 and at the same time the Oxenholme to Kendal and Windermere line went into operation. Three months later the Shap section of the Lancaster and Carlisle Railway was opened.

The first continuous rail links between Scotland's two principal cities (Edinburgh and Glasgow) and London were forged by the opening of the Caledonian Railway's Beattock to Carlisle section in September 1847 and the Beattock to Glasgow and Edinburgh in February 1848.

On the East Coast route to Scotland a temporary bridge was opened over the Tyne in October 1848. Robert Stephenson's High Level Bridge at Newcastle-upon-Tyne was completed in 1849 and with the opening of his Royal Border Bridge at Berwick in 1850 a second Anglo-Scottish route was opened. At that date, however, East Coast trains still ran from Euston via Rugby and thence over the various lines controlled by George Hudson, an entrepreneur from the Midlands, northwards to Berwick.

left:
The high level bridge at
Newcastle-upon-Tyne.
From *The Illustrated London
News*. (Colourviews
Picture Library)

Portrait of a Railway Baron,
George Hudson.
(Colourviews Picture
Library)

Hudson, a native of York, was one of the first to exploit the railways in the pursuit of personal power, prestige and fortune. His business life had started with a drapery shop but a legacy of £30,000 enabled him to buy his way into the world of railway finance. A tough individualist, he had the money and soon bought the influence which opened up the corridors of power to him and found him seats on the boards of companies. His toughness made him ideal as a 'trouble-shooter' and soon he was attaining company chairmanships as well as the office of Lord Mayor of York in 1837 and he became a Member of Parliament for Sunderland in 1845. One of his chairmanships was of the York and North Midland which had been formed to link York with the London to Leeds lines at Altofts Junction. Not content with this, Hudson went on to lease the Leeds and Selby

Railway in 1840. He thereupon removed most of its passenger services so that travellers were forced to go via Methley and his own York and North Midland.

Having secured control of railway traffic between the West Riding and York and Humberside, Hudson went on to increase his power by promoting schemes to extend the Great North of England from Darlington to Newcastle. He hoped to reach agreement with the Stockton and Darlington for a line-sharing arrangement but failed and so drove his line at right angles through the S & D at Darlington. This strange flat 'junction' of the two lines lasted well into this century.

It was Hudson who secured for the North British Railway the right to build the line from Edinburgh to Berwick. Thereafter,

An early Royal saloon: a Southampton Railway vehicle of 1844. From the *Illustrated London News.* (Colourviews Picture Library)

right:
A contemporary drawing of Bristol Temple Meads station 1846. (Crown Copyright National Railway Museum).

completion of the two Robert Stephenson bridges we have mentioned over the Tweed and Tyne completed the East Coast link between London and Scotland. Not content with his undoubted power in his native northlands, however, Hudson also gained the support of shareholders of the North Midland (as opposed to the York & North Midland) and they voted him into the chairmanship.

In 1844 he was the prime mover of the amalgamation of the North Midland, the Midland Counties and the Birmingham & Derby Junction into the Midland Railway. All three of these railways met at Derby and NM had been in furious competition with the Midland Counties and the Birmingham & Derby to attract customers for through passage to London. As an example of the fare-cutting, the 38-mile journey from Derby to Hampton-in-Arden cost only one shilling (5p).

Though Hudson's motives can be questioned in a number of his dealings, it has to be admitted that others were to be of considerable benefit to company shareholders. His successful appeals to investors in those three companies to sink their differences was an example of this. It also, of course, gave him rule over routes extending from Bristol and Rugby to Edinburgh! Not for nothing was he known as the Railway King.

However, his reign was nearing its end. The existing rail route from London Euston to York ran mainly over lines which he controlled. Not surprisingly he therefore bitterly opposed proposals for a direct line from London to York. This time, though, he was over-ruled and the Great Northern Railway gained permission to open a route from Askern, near Doncaster, to London via Retford, Lincoln, Boston and Peterborough. Between Askern and York the company used the tracks of the Lancashire & Yorkshire Railway to Knottingley, where there was a junction with the York & North Midland. The London terminus at Maiden Lane was a temporary one. It served from August 1850 until October 1852, when Kings Cross was brought into use following completion in August of the direct line from Peterborough to Retford. In the interim a detour had been made via Lincoln.

The fact that it was possible for the Great Northern to reach York over one of the lines controlled by Hudson – the York & North Midland – was an indication of his diminishing power. The great railway rush was slowing and the value of railway shares had fallen. As always in such circumstances, questions were then raised about Hudson's management of the finances of various companies and in 1849 shareholders of the Eastern Counties Railway vocally chastised

Crewe station and works (in distance) from a contemporary drawing 1848. (Crown Copyright National Railway Museum)

below:
Kings Cross station train shed 1851. From *The Illustrated London News*. (Colourviews Picture Library)

him. Next it was discovered that the value of shares in his companies had been maintained by paying dividends out of capital. In April Hudson resigned his chairmanship of the Midland Railway and a subsequent committee of inquiry found that the Railway King had 'abused the confidence that was placed in him by wielding the power he obtained to forward his own interest'. Nevertheless, Hudson had made an undoubted contribution to the establishment of a viable railway system and he has a just memorial in Hudson House, British Rail's Eastern Region headquarters in York.

Parliament had always shown a preference for a larger number of companies competing against each other but Hudson's successful amalgamation to form the Midland Railway broke this pattern. The Grand Junction Railway took over the Liverpool & Manchester in 1845 and in the following year the London and North Western Railway was formed by the amalgamation of the Grand Junction, London & Birmingham and the Manchester & Birmingham, opened

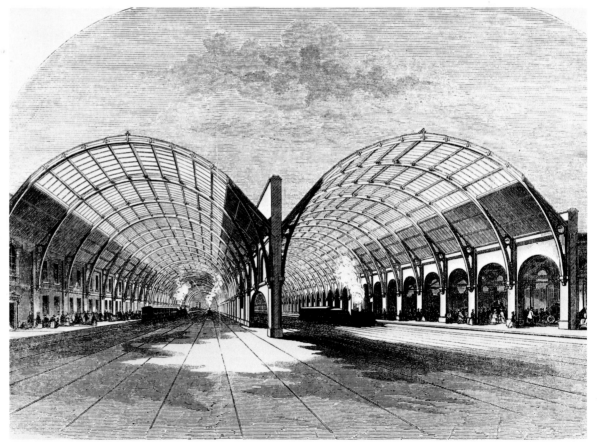

only four years previously between Manchester and Crewe. (Birmingham was reached over Grand Junction tracks.)

The Grand Junction took with it into the new company – destined to be for a time the world's largest joint stock company – some sections of the West Coast route to Scotland north of the Liverpool & Manchester line. In 1859 the Lancaster and Preston Junction and the Lancaster and Carlisle Railways were leased to the LNWR and were vested in that company in 1879.

A similar process of acquisition and amalgamation led to the formation in 1854 of the North Eastern Railway to establish a major company for the East Coast route. The main constituents of the NER were the York, Newcastle & Berwick, the York & North Midland and the Leeds Northern.

Parliament continued to exercise control over the formation of new railway companies, which still required an Act. Though there had been disquiet over the size of the new LNWR it had eventually been granted the necessary Act. However, when the Midland Railway later wanted to amalgamate or 'co-operate' with the LNWR and sought Parliamentary approval in 1869, it was refused. Instead the Midland approached the Great Northern, which agreed that its trains could use Kings Cross as its London terminus, running in on the line from Hitchin. This resulted in proposals for a Midland/Great Northern merger, but again Parliament opposed the idea, which was dropped.

Even so, acquisition and mergers continued among the small companies to set the pattern for Britain's railway system which was to remain almost unchanged until the 'Grouping' of companies after World War I. Whereas the Industrial Revolution was started in some countries by the emergence of the railways, in Britain it was the railways which accelerated the revolution and fed upon the expanding markets which it had provided for travel and transport of freight.

The railways were quick to see the advantages of cheap return tickets, particularly at holiday periods which had now established a new pattern of movement by the populace to the expanding 'holiday resorts'. Since trains on which cheap fares were obtainable were frequently overcrowded, it was a natural development for firms or organisations to want to reserve complete trains for their members. The pioneer in this new market for the chartered train was Thomas Cook with his special train from Leicester to Loughborough which took a party of about 1000 temperance reformers on an excursion on 5 July 1841. Cheap tickets to the Continent were first offered by the South Eastern Railway in 1848 and Thomas Cook began organising

Britannia Bridge, built in 1850, was Robert Stephenson's masterpiece of tubular construction linking Anglesey with the mainland. From *The Illustrated London News*. (Colourviews Picture Library)

left:
The Royal Border Bridge at Berwick-on-Tweed, designed by Robert Stephenson took a little over three years to build. From *The Illustrated London News*. (Colourviews Picture Library)

Continental holidays in 1855.

The Great Exhibition at the Crystal Palace in Hyde Park, London in 1851 prompted one of the first large-scale organised movements of passengers by rail. One-million people a month visited the exhibition during the six months it was open and they travelled to London very largely by train from all parts of the country and from the sea ports whence they had arrived from overseas. Excursion fares were available for as little as five shillings (25p) return between Manchester or Leeds and London. For the International Exhibition in Paris in 1867 Cook arranged excursions for working men which cost only 34 shillings (£1.70) for four days.

Having at first treated third-class passengers as little more than cattle, the railways now did all they could to attract the working classes to take advantage of their concessionary fares. In 1844 they had been offended by Gladstone's Act which required them to run what became known as 'Parliamentary trains' with proper seating (wooden benches), protection from the weather and fares of not more than one penny a mile for third-class passengers. By the 1850s the companies realized that the policy of encouraging mass travel by offering cheap fares was paying dividends. In fact by 1880 third-class travel accounted for almost 38 per cent of receipts and a decade later the receipts exceeded those for first- and second-class tickets. Even so, little attempt was made to improve third-class accommodation until the middle of the 1870s when the Midland Railway led the way by introducing padded seats and proper compartments instead of shoulder-high wooden partitions. Even then, it was another 20 years before these improvements became widespread.

The companies attempted not only to attract the custom of the working classes on holiday, they also set about providing services to convey working people to and from their places of employment.

The *Fairfield* steam carriage built for the Eastern Counties Railway in 1848. A similar (but 7′ 0″ gauge) vehicle was constructed for the Bristol and Exeter Railway – both were by Adams & Co. (P B Whitehouse collection)

below & right:
Eastern Counties Railway 1847 interiors of 1st and 2nd class compartments. From the *Illustrated London News*. (Colourviews Picture Library)

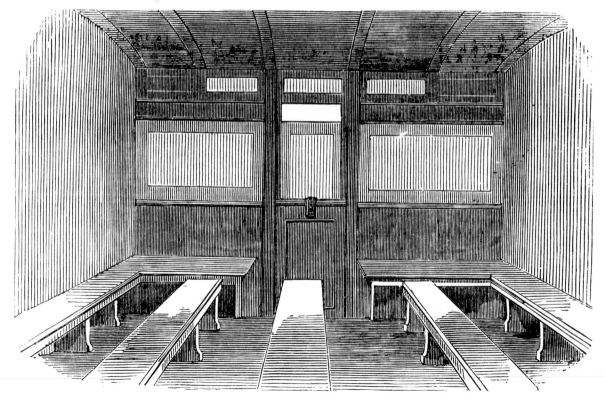

The coming of railways to the towns had the effect of prompting many middle class families to move to the outskirts or even into more rural surroundings from where the head of the family would commute by train. The physical act of carving the rail routes into the towns also had another effect: much housing was demolished, particularly in working-class areas, and workmen who had previously lived close to their places of work had also to move further away and travel by train daily. The railway companies offered special cheap-rate workmen's trains which, in turn, encouraged the growth of new suburbs. More than this, the needs of railways themselves also led to the growth of 'railway towns' such as Swindon and Wolverton. The former was a small market town until the Great Western Railway chose it as the site for its locomotive and carriage works. By 1851 92 per cent of Swindon's population were employed in the railway workshops. Wolverton was chosen by the London & Birmingham Railway for its locomotive works because it was approximately mid-way along the line and was close to the Grand Junction Canal. By 1851 85 per cent of the population worked for the railway. Similarly other towns grew because they became railway junctions.

The railways were thus playing an important role in re-shaping the whole life of the country, socially, commercially, and even topographically.

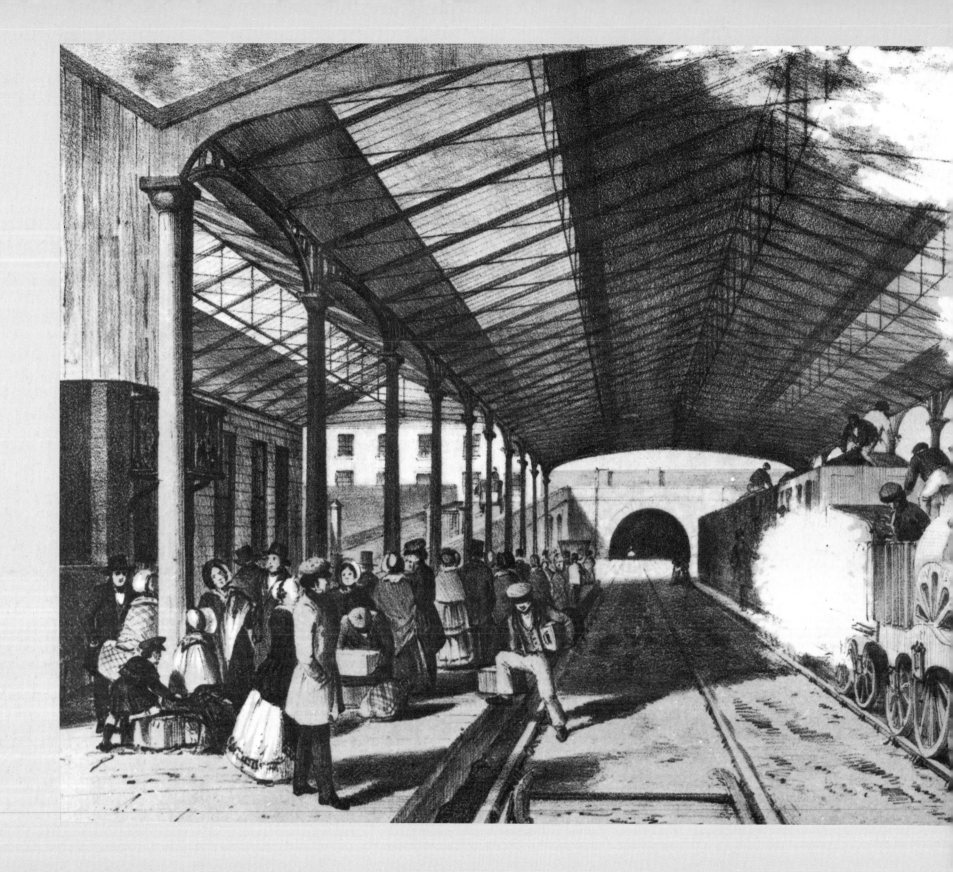

2
GROWTH AND DEVELOPMENT

EARLY LOCOMOTIVES, TRAINS AND SIGNALS

Despite the twenty-five years of pioneering development between Trevithick's first railway locomotive and the Rainhill trials in 1829, the shape of locomotives and the arrangement of essential components continued very much on a 'hit-or-miss' basis for several years after the trials.

George Stephenson's 'stable' of engines for the Stockton & Darlington which followed the *Rocket* were broadly similar but they did not have its high, steeply inclined cylinders. Instead, the cylinders were lowered and their angle altered so that they lay almost horizontally as it was thought that the original arrangement caused unsteady motion.

The first locomotive on which the cylinders were placed between the frames below the smokebox and forward of the driving wheels rather than behind them was Robert Stephenson's *Planet*. This engine, which had one pair of leading carrying wheels and one pair of driving wheels, was of 2–2–0 configuration whereas *Rocket* was an 0–2–2. It was delivered from the Stephenson works in Newcastle to the Liverpool & Manchester Railway only a month after the company had begun its service in September 1830.

Robert Stephenson achieved the objective of spreading the weight which necessarily went with increased power by using more axles. He did so with his *Patentee* of 1834, which was a 2–2–2 with one driving axle behind two carrying axles. Though the London & Birmingham continued to use 2–2–0s and 0–4–0s until 1845, *Patentee* was to establish a successful basis on which Stephenson and other builders could rely for future developments.

Meanwhile the Great Western Railway, with its 7ft 0¼in broad gauge, was adopting a locomotive building practice which was soon to become widespread. Other railways had ordered locomotives from specialist builders almost 'off the shelf', choosing available types which seemed to suit their needs. Daniel Gooch, who had been appointed GWR Locomotive Superintendent in 1837 – just before his twenty-first birthday – was not impressed by the design or performance of some of the locomotives which had been ordered before his arrival. He eventually decided to lay down his own specifications.

Among the engines which had been ordered prior to his appointment had been two from the Stephenson works at Newcastle where he had been employed. These 2–2–2s, *North Star* and *Morning Star*, had originally been ordered for the 5ft 6in gauge New Orleans Railway but the contract had been cancelled. They were converted to broad gauge for the GWR in 1837 and provided the young Gooch with his first reliable locomotives. Ten more, all bearing Star names, were bought by the company. Other generally similar 2–2–2s were ordered from different builders and later, engines of the

This photograph of the preserved 0–4–2 *Lion* was taken during the filming of the *Titfield Thunderbolt* – a well-known Ealing Studios comedy of the mid-1950s. (P M Alexander)

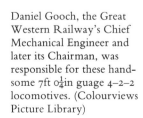

The celebration to commemorate the centenary of the Liverpool & Manchester Railway in 1930 included the refurbishing and steaming of the *Lion* coupled to three first-class and three third-class replica coaches – a scenario repeated over 40 years later in the spring of 1980 during the RAIL 150 celebrations. (Cecil J Allen collection)

78mph. *Great Western*'s average of 67mph was achieved when the locomotive was hauling a load of 60 tons over a distance of 53 miles. The performance was so spectacular that doubt was later cast on its feasibility. However, analysis of the known facts and technical data showed that a train of this power/weight ratio (around $4\frac{1}{2}$hp/ton) could have achieved such a performance. In 1848 GWR trains were regularly running the 53 miles from London to Didcot in between 48 and 50 minutes. *Great Western*, which came out in 1846, was followed by a few more 2–2–2s but then Gooch switched to a 4–2–2 configuration in 1847 with the Iron Dukes. Though by later standards these might appear to have been comparatively crude locomotives they proved eminently suited to travel at high speeds, hauling light loads along the superbly designed London-Bristol route engineered by Brunel. The Iron Dukes, of which 29 were built, had large boilers and fireboxes, 8ft diameter driving wheels and short piston strokes. With an all-up weight of 53 tons, they continued in production until 1855. By that time the pattern for the higher inter-city rail speeds of this century had been established, thanks to the combination of Gooch's engines and Brunel's broad gauge.

2–4–0 and 0–6–0 types were ordered for freight working. Some of the early 2–2–2s were converted to 4–2–2 tank engines and used on branch lines for many years.

The first of the engines built to Gooch's specifications to emerge from the GWR works at Swindon was the 2–2–2 *Great Western*, which was later to distinguish itself by running at an average speed of over 55mph on the round trip from Paddington to Exeter via Bristol and averaged 67mph between Paddington and Didcot during the gauge trials to which we have already referred. On a falling gradient of 1-in-100 one 4–2–2 had already attained a speed of

While the speed on the broad gauge was steadily increased, the smaller locomotives on the standard gauge could not match the GWR's performance, despite experiments with a number of designs intended to obtain greater power. There was a great fear that larger and higher boilers would induce engines to overturn if they were used on frames built for the narrower standard gauge. One attempt to lower the centre of gravity by matching a low-slung boiler with large driving wheels was made by Thomas Russell Crampton. He

Daniel Gooch, the Great Western Railway's Chief Mechanical Engineer and later its Chairman, was responsible for these handsome 7ft 0$\frac{1}{4}$in guage 4–2–2 locomotives. (Colourviews Picture Library)

Anna Zinkeisen's painting of a Stockton & Darlington Railway train. Note the first class coach after the fashion of a stage coach, the second class barely covered, the flat wagon for carrying private vehicles and the third class open to all the elements. (Colourviews Picture Library)

right:
Kept to run one of the Director's saloons on the LNWR, this strange single wheeler survives today in the National Collection. No 3020 Cornwall is shown here 'at home' in Crewe Works. (John Adams)

patented a locomotive on which the driving axle and big driving wheels were located *behind* the boiler at the extreme rear, with only small carrying wheels beneath the boiler. Although Crampton's design achieved considerable success on the continent, it was not a high-speed locomotive and though stable it ran hard on the track. However it was a Crampton engine which probably came closest to broad-gauge standards of speed at that time when it ran the 41 miles from Wolverhampton to Coventry in 42 minutes.

Robert Stephenson also brought out a variation in design with his 4–2–0 'long boiler'. It was intended to increase thermal efficiency by making better use of the fuel through the increased heating surface of the longer tubes in the boiler, which also reduced the emission of hot cinders. For operating reasons the wheelbase had to be short. All the wheels were, therefore, placed in front of the firebox. As a result there was an overhang at the rear and this made the engine sway at speeds which would have resulted in considerable wear on the back wheels and could have caused accidents.

The largest wheel diameter ever employed on the standard gauge was the 8ft 6in of *Cornwall*, the famous engine built at Crewe in 1847 by Frances Trevithick, eldest son of Richard, for the LNWR. The boiler was slung below the driving axle, which passed through a channel formed in the top of the boiler. The rear carrying axle ran through the firebox in a transverse tube. In 1858, having put up no exceptional performances, *Cornwall* was rebuilt from a 4–2–2 to a

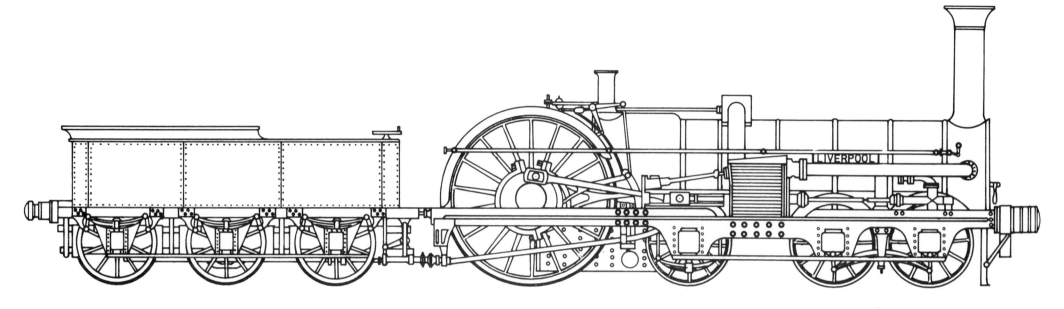

conventional 2–2–2 with the boiler above the driving axle. It now performed better than its original configuration, though no better than other LNWR 2–2–2s with 7ft 6in diameter wheels. *Cornwall* is preserved in the National Railway Museum at York.

The designer for E B Wilson & Company of Leeds, David Joy, came out with a variation on the 2–2–2 which was to lead to future development. In 1846 he produced a 2–2–2 for the London, Brighton and South Coast Railway which had a fairly long wheelbase and 6ft diameter driving wheels set outside the frames and carrying wheels inside. This locomotive, named *Jenny Lind* after the contemporary Swedish soprano, had a boiler pressure of 120lb/sq in – unusually high for that period. The name was used for numerous successors and two of these went to the London & North Western Railway. Here they suggested to J E McConnell, the LNWR's Locomotive Superintendent, the idea of carrying *all* the wheels outside the frame. His first 2–2–2s from the company's Wolverton locomotive works came out in 1851 and, like the *Jenny Lind*s, had a long wheelbase. All the wheels were outside the frame. The exposed position of the 7ft drivers earned the engines the sobriquet 'Bloomers' (from the contemporary reformer of women's dress whose designs revealed that women had legs!). Further 'Bloomers' were produced with driving wheels of various diameters; they had a boiler pressure of 150lb/sq in and served the LNWR long and well in fast passenger traffic.

In response to a demand by the directors of the LNWR for the

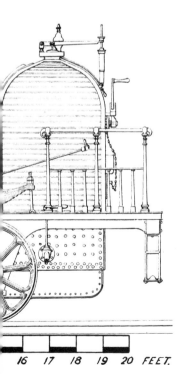

16 17 18 19 20 FEET.

company to have locomotives capable of covering the journey from London to Birmingham in two hours, McConnell produced his Patent class of 2–2–2 in the early 1850s. These had 7ft 6in driving wheels and were criticized for their high centre of gravity. In fact their weaker feature proved to be the complicated boiler with a very large fire grate which McConnell intended to burn coal in place of the more expensive coke generally used. Eventually a brick arch and deflector plate were built into the firebox to provide an effective answer to the problem of size. The addition of the arch and downward-sloping deflector inside the firebox door ensured that air entering through the gate or firedoor remained in contact with the fire for as long as possible before reaching the boiler tubes. The arch was first used in 1850. Matthew Kirtley, Mechanical Engineer of the Midland Railway, later began experiments which proved the efficacy of the principle in 1859, after which time the arch and deflector plate became standard features of the steam locomotive's combustion system.

Like David Joy and McConnell, A Sturrock of the Great Northern also adopted high-boiler pressure. He built an experimental 4–2–2 which, though it had 7ft 6in driving wheels, strongly resembled Gooch's broad-gauge single-drivers. It had a boiler pressure of 150lb/sq in but did not put up any exceptional performances.

Another development which later became standard steam locomotion practice took place in the 1840s and involved the variable valve gear to control the distribution of steam to the cylinders. Devised at the Stephensons' works in 1841, it was called Stephenson's link motion. The refinement was an articulated linkage by means of which the travel of the valve could be varied and thus also the proportion of the piston stroke during which steam was admitted to the cylinders. For peak efficiency the admission period needed to be kept short so that steam already in the cylinder when the valve closed continued to work by expanding. In 1849 the Walschaerts valve gear linkage was introduced and remained in common use to the end of steam, its pattern of external rods and cranks easily recognised by enthusiasts.

During the first 20 years or so of railways in Britain, development work was not confined to improving the locomotives or to finding stronger, more reliable materials for the track. The railway was a new concept relying on much new technology but it also made use initially of existing transport practices, adapting them as necessary. The builders of the first railway coaches, for example, had a ready-made prototype in the stage or mail carriages of the road. Road coaches usually had four seats inside and bench seats at the front and back of the roof, outside, which took a further ten people. Luggage was held on a rack on the roof while the mail and valuables were carried in a boot on the back.

The greater haulage capability of the steam locomotive meant that more people could be carried and the first railway coaches were built in the form of three or four road-style coaches mounted on a common frame. The broad gauge made it possible to seat eight passengers in a Great Western coach and even the standard gauge coaches were able to take six instead of four people in each section or compartment. Even so, the early carriages were only about six feet wide and they were for first-class passengers only. Some had a box seat for the guard and, like the road coaches, were fitted with rails round the roof so that luggage could be stowed there. To add extra brake power to that of the engine and tender, guards worked the handbrakes fitted to their own coaches.

From 1837 mail was carried by the railways and in 1838 the London & Birmingham Railway introduced a special coach for Post Office traffic with first-class passenger accommodation inside and the mail carried in boxes on the roof. Some coaches incorporated what looked like a projecting 'boot' at one end; rather than for stowing luggage, it was to enable a passenger lying on a paddle board across the seats to stretch his legs. The compartments were only five feet from side to side so that a passenger could not lie down unless there was this extra boot space. A coach of this type was used by the Dowager Queen Adelaide in 1842 and is now preserved in the National Railway Museum.

Second-class passengers who would have travelled on the roofs of road coaches – and could do so on a railway coach up to at least 1840 – were provided with the most basic of accommodation. Though the wagons were roofed they were usually open-sided so that even those passengers lucky enough to have a side wheel next to them still had to suffer the draughts. Third-class passengers were not catered for by some companies and by those who did carry them they were treated little better than animals, riding in open wagons which might, if they were lucky, have bench seats. Holes drilled in the floor prevented accumulations of water in wet weather but that was small comfort to passengers who were probably wet through anyway.

Legislation eventually improved the lot of all, but particularly the third-class passengers. A Select Committee of 1839 inquired into 'the state of communication by railway' and as a result the Regulation of Railway Acts of 1840 and 1842 established rules for the inspection of lines, safety in general and the fixing of fares. The Board of Trade in future included a Railway Department under an Inspector General of Railways. In 1844 Parliament insisted that third-class passengers must be catered for by all companies; the Regulations of Railways Act of that year laid down that at least one train in each direction every day on each line should provide third-class accommodation in closed carriages (roofed and glazed) with seats. The Act, which became known as the 'Cheap Trains Act', also stipulated that trains were to pick up and set down at every station and that their speed must be at least 12mph. The fare was not to exceed one penny per

Each railway company had its own seal, often a decorative one. These reproductions show typical seals of early railways before their amalgamation into larger companies. (British Railways and Colourviews Picture Library)

Virtually all the pre-Grouping railways carried their own crests or coats of arms either on the locomotive and/or coaches. These examples show garters, crests and coats of arms of the Glasgow & South Western, Highland, South Eastern & Chatham and Great Northern Railways. (Colourviews Picture Library)

mile. To mark their objection some companies ran the trains at inconvenient times.

By this time second-class coaches had glazed windows and some padding on seats. First-class compartments had plush interiors, padded cushions, partitions and curtains. The third-class accommodation for the 'Parliamentary trains' marked a considerable improvement: coaches were usually four-wheelers, often very well protected from the weather because there were few windows, had wooden bench seats but otherwise bare interiors without partitions.

As traffic increased it became necessary to control the movement of trains. Fortunately, electrical science was developing at the same time as the railways. Though the electric telegraph was demonstrated

A model of a Bristol &
Exeter Railway 7ft 0¼in
gauge 4–2–2. The engine
dates from 1849, was rebuilt
in 1866 and became GWR
No 2012. (Colourviews
Picture Library)

left:
Government regulations of
1844 required companies to
run at least one train a day
over their routes with fares
at one penny per mile. These
'Parliamentary' trains with
their uncomfortable third
class vehicles were often run
at inconvenient hours and at
very slow speeds. This
drawing shows the interior
of a typical third class coach
in 1858. (Colourviews
Picture Library)

between Euston Station and Camden in 1838 it was not widely used for some years, either because staff were not literate enough to use it or because companies could see no financial advantage. Later its principles were widely used to provide signalmen with a means of communicating details of train movements. Signalling was rudimentary initially, generally relying on men described as 'policemen' to give hand signals to drivers indicating whether they must stop, slow down or proceed at full speed. The railway police were also responsible for the security of lines and stations.

Mechanical signalling methods gradually took over from hands and flags. They were usually worked by policemen stationed at individual signals. One of the earliest and most recognisable as the forefather of the railway signal (used universally before coloured lights became common) was introduced on the Liverpool & Manchester Railway in 1834. It was a red-painted swivelling board which was turned to face the driver of an oncoming train if it had to stop, and aligned edge-on if the line was clear. Edge-on the board was barely visible from a distance, thereby complying with the early principle that absence of a signal indicated a clear track. In time,

however, it was realised that a definite 'clear-track' signal was desirable and in 1838 the GWR introduced a swivelling signal with a disc and a crossbar mounted at right angles to each other. Positive danger was indicated by the bar being face on, clear by the disc face on. Since there was still no communication between stations the 'clear' indication was no absolute guarantee of an open line ahead.

With individually controlled signals a train was, at first, allowed to proceed if the policeman judged that sufficient time had elapsed since the last train had gone ahead. In some cases policemen were instructed to stop fast trains and tell the driver how long it had been since the last train had passed. This put the onus on the driver to regulate his speed. Such an imprecise system could be dispensed with when the electric telegraph was introduced. A signalman – the policemen's duties were soon split between men specialising in particular jobs – could ask his colleague along the line whether the previous train had reached or passed the next signalling point and whether the next train could proceed. The line was divided into sections with a signalman at both ends and only one train was allowed on each section at a time. The 'block section' system, as it was called, came into use on some lines in the early 1840s.

The next step from a signalman patrolling the signals and points under his control to operate them individually was to bring the means of operation together in his shelter. The shelter developed into the signalbox and as more levers working signals and points came under the control of one man, methods were devised to guard against conflicting signals being displayed. It was, for example, essential to ensure that if points and signals had been set to clear one route, the levers controlling signals and points on a converging route were locked to danger. Such equipment was first seen in primitive form in the 1840s. In the same decade came the semaphore signal, with an arm held horizontally for danger and inclined down 45 degrees for caution and vertically down for clear.

As main lines were built throughout the country, stations were erected to serve towns and villages along the routes, or even merely close to them. Many country stations had sidings for goods traffic so that freight could be sent to places that, before the railway came, could only be reached by horse-drawn wagon. By the middle of the nineteenth century railways were becoming established as part of everyday life. Long journeys could now be measured in terms of hours rather than days and goods had a countrywide distribution network. In just a few years a way of life that had lasted for centuries had been changed forever.

THE NETWORK DEVELOPS-
THE INDEPENDENT
COMPANIES

The second half of the nineteenth century was marked by the virtual completion of the British railway map with infilling by more main lines, cross-country routes and branch lines. There were also the development of railway empires, ruthless competition between companies providing rival services over similar routes, and the emergence of strong-willed personalities who led those companies.

The London & North Western Railway rose to a dominant position by further acquisitions after its formation from the amalgamation of the London & Birmingham, the Grand Junction and the Manchester & Birmingham railways. It encouraged and supported acquisitions by other companies if these were thought to be to the LNWR's advantage, and prompted nominally independent companies to keep intruders out of North Western territory. It pressed the Chester & Holyhead Railway to speed up its construction work so that the LNWR could secure the Irish Mail traffic and prevent the GWR from winning the traffic for its own service via Fishguard. The Chester & Holyhead was taken over by the LNWR in 1858.

Euston was regarded by the LNWR as the 'Gateway to the North' and the Great Northern's projected line to London was seen as a threat of serious competition for traffic between London and the North of England. Already in existence was the LNWR's own route from Euston to the Midlands, Yorkshire and the North East by way of Rugby. However, despite LNWR opposition, the Great Northern reached its first London terminus at Maiden Lane in 1850.

Led by its General Manager, Captain Mark Huish, the LNWR also obstructed the Great Western Railway in its bid to extend north-westwards from Banbury to Birmingham, Chester and Merseyside. The Shrewsbury & Chester and Shrewsbury & Birmingham companies fought against the obstruction in alliance with the GWR but the other line involved, that from Birkenhead to Chester, had already become a satellite of the LNWR and in 1850 it was persuaded by devious and underhand means to handle Shrewsbury & Chester traffic. The GWR and the Shrewsbury companies responded by obtaining running powers over the Birkenhead line

by Act of Parliament in 1851. When, encouraged by the LNWR, the Birkenhead company sought to withdraw from the agreement, Parliament intervened again. At last it was clear that the powerful LNWR alliance could be challenged successfully.

The meandering route of the GWR (the 'Great Way Round', according to cynics) to Exeter via Bristol left a big area further south open to railway development. The London & South Western Railway had extended in 1847 from Bishopstoke (Eastleigh) to Salisbury, which was later to be on its main line to the West Country. In the late 1840s, however, the company planned to serve Exeter via Dorchester and opened the Southampton & Dorchester Railway the same year as the Salisbury branch. The Southampton & Dorchester was planned as a broad-gauge line by local businessmen who

Crewe 1865 looking back towards the station from the locomotive works. (Crown Copyright National Railway Museum)

right:
Brighton terminus 1862 – note the ornate station roof, the slotted post signals and the 'birdcage' roof (for the guard's lookout) on the four-wheeled coaches centre left and right. (National Railway Museum)

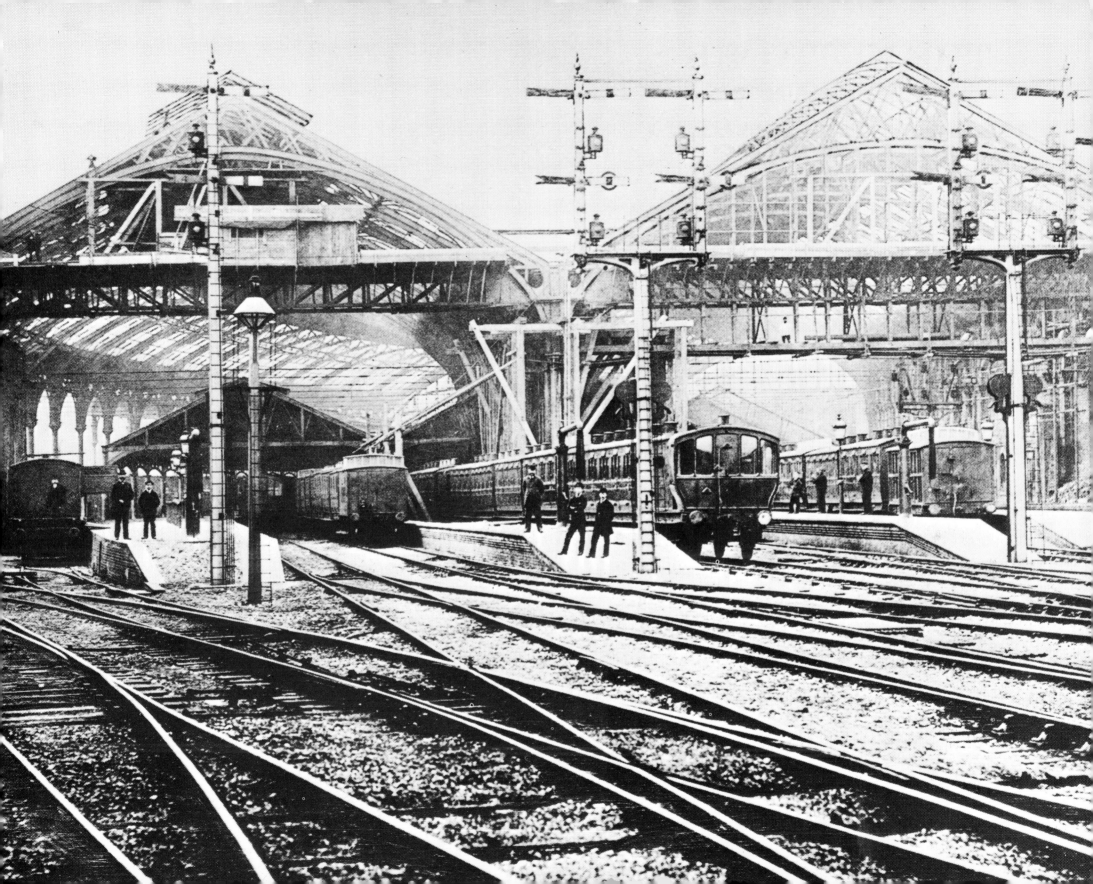

An interesting example of a locomotive built by an outside firm of contractors for a railway but not delivered to them. LB&SCR No 219 was built by Manning Wardle in 1866 – the original order was from the Cambrian Railway. (Colourviews Picture Library)

had originally intended to lease it to the GWR. However, as the result of a deal between the GWR and LSWR, it went to the latter. In return the LSWR agreed to leave railway development in west Cornwall to the GWR. The London & South Western extended its service to Weymouth from Dorchester in 1857 by obtaining running powers over GWR tracks, while GWR trains continued to serve Dorchester via Swindon and Westbury.

The West of England main line from Reading to Exeter via Newbury and Westbury, with a junction for Yeovil and Dorchester at Castle Cary, was formed from a number of minor lines and was not completed until 1906. The route to Exeter opened by the LSWR in July 1860 was from a junction with the Southampton line west of Basingstoke, through Salisbury and Honiton. Overcoming numerous objections and obstructions the LSWR went beyond Exeter north of Dartmoor and down to Plymouth. It opened a through service from London Waterloo to that city in 1876 and completed its penetration of the area with the opening of its line to Padstow on 27 March 1899.

The GWR and LSWR covered individual areas west of Plymouth but for traffic between Plymouth and Exeter and on to London, particularly for Atlantic liners calling at Plymouth, the two companies ran fast overnight trains. Both also developed important

holiday traffic, the GWR to resorts west of Exeter and the LSWR to north Cornwall and places on the south Devon coast east of Exeter which were not served by the GWR.

South of London the LSWR competed with the London, Brighton and South Coast Railway for Portsmouth and Isle of Wight traffic. When the first LSWR trains tried to get through in January 1859 there were fights at Havant. The LBSCR also competed with the South Eastern Railway for traffic on routes along the Kent and Sussex borders.

Sir Edward Watkin, Chairman of the South Eastern at the time, had earlier played a large part in the sale of the Trent Valley Railway in Staffordshire, of which he was Secretary, to the LNWR, the board of which he also joined. In 1853 Watkin became General Manager of the Manchester, Sheffield & Lincolnshire Railway. There he gradually loosened the company's ties with the LNWR and worked up a closer relationship with the Great Northern. He became Chairman of the MS & LR in 1864 and worked vigorously to fulfil his ambition to bring the Sheffield-based company to London. That, however, took nearly 30 years and a long Parliamentary struggle before a Bill for the London extension received the Royal assent in 1893. Meanwhile, Watkin had become Chairman of the South Eastern Railway in 1866 and of the Metropolitan Railway

right:
A print from the *Illustrated London News* of 1868 showing the Midland Railway station at Leeds looking from Holbeck junction. (Colourviews Picture Library)

right:
Furness Railway's 2–4–0
No 2 of class E1. These
engines were built by Sharp
Stewart & Company in 1870
and subsequently rebuilt as
shown here in 1896. (P B
Whitehouse collection)

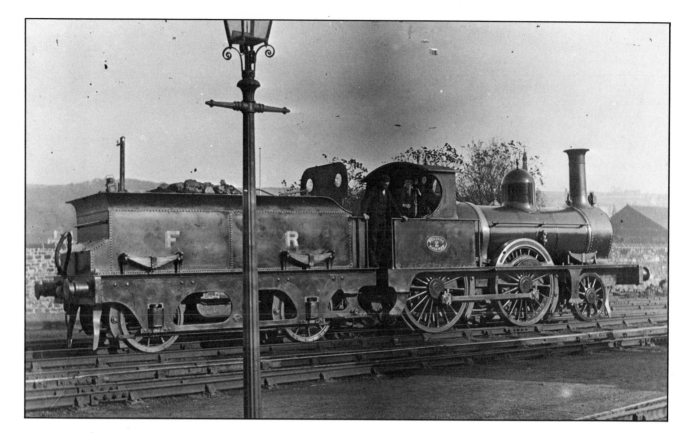

The Great Northern
Railway's main line at
Hitchin station looking south
circa 1870. Note the
condition of the track even
though this was a main
trunk route to Scotland.
(C J Allen Collection)

in 1872. He also took an interest in the newly formed Channel Tunnel company. Collectively these wide interests made possible the eventual through-running of trains between Manchester and the Channel ports, via the Metropolitan, the East London and the South Eastern railways, and – given a Channel tunnel – on to the Continent. However, the grand dream of a Manchester-Paris express was not to become reality. Watkin resigned all his chairmanships because of ill health only a year after the Manchester, Sheffield & Lincolnshire Railway's extension to London received approval. Watkin's withdrawal brought to an end much of the inter-company squabbling which, while it achieved some worthwhile results, had delayed some important developments.

Even so, while these battles had been going on, extensions of railway service were carried out elsewhere in the British Isles. Cambrian Railways, for example, had a main line crossing Wales from Welshpool to Barmouth and Aberystwyth, and a branch southwards from Moat Lane Junction to Brecon, where it joined the Brecon & Methyr line from over the border. The North Wales coast was served by the LNWR while South and West Wales were GWR territory. There were also various small companies linking the coal mines of the South Wales valleys with the steelworks and ports. As Welsh industry expanded the LNWR made further inroads, serving isolated areas in South Wales reached by jointly worked lines and also obtaining running powers to major centres, even to Swansea, Llandrindod Wells and Llanwrtyd Wells.

The early advance of railways in East Anglia was a slow process, dogged by low traffic and a shortage of capital. Moreover, the first company to turn its attentions north-eastwards from London, the Eastern Counties Railway, caused itself added problems by adopting a track gauge of 5ft. It took some years to realise the error of its ways and convert to standard gauge. By the time the ECR reached Colchester in 1843, another company, the Eastern Union, had stepped in and completed a line to Norwich. The ECR was naturally furious and for five years it persistently created difficulties at Colchester, where the two companies' trains connected. In 1854 it took over the EUR. Meanwhile, in 1845, the ECR also reached Norwich over an easier route via Cambridge and Ely. In 1846 it proposed a branch from Ely to Peterborough, intending to establish its own London–York route, but Parliament decided that the Great Northern Railway's scheme should go ahead instead.

The Great Eastern Railway's London terminus, Liverpool Street, which opened in stages between 1874 and 1875, eventually became

Here is Bridgend station in South Wales in the later days of the 7ft 0¼in gauge, 1878. (National Railway Museum)

below:
Victorian country station: Market Bosworth station Leicestershire) in 1883 with Midland Railway single-wheeler 2–2–2 No 35 (shedded at Coalville) in the platform. (R E Tustin collection)

The Great Western Railway's tunnel under the river Severn greatly reduced the distance and therefore the train times to South Wales. Construction of this masterpiece in civil engineering began in 1875 and the work was completed in 1886. (National Railway Museum)

another starting point for the north as well as for East Anglia. The Great Eastern was created in 1862 by mergers of the East Anglian companies and their various offshoots which ran inland and to coastal towns such as Harwich and Yarmouth. Between 1879 and 1882 the Great Eastern agreed to operate jointly with the Great Northern on a cross-country route from March, near Ely, to Doncaster via Spalding, Sleaford, Lincoln and Gainsborough. When the North Eastern granted the GER running powers north of Doncaster, the Great Eastern was able to establish a through express passenger service from Liverpool Street to York.

In 1876 a third Anglo-Scottish main line was opened, extending the influence of the Midland Railway from South Wales to the Clyde Valley. Despite earlier quarrels the Great Northern allowed the Midland access to Kings Cross via a GNR line from Leicester to Hitchin which had opened in 1857, but the GNR would not allow

Midland Railway trains to use the track from Hitchin into Kings Cross at the expense of its own services. The Midland endured the difficulties thus created until 1863, when it gained Parliamentary approval to build a new line from Bedford via St Albans into St Pancras terminus, opened in 1868.

The next Midland Railway goal was Manchester, which presented the challenge of beating the LNWR for London business. In 1867 the Midland opened an extension to Manchester of its Ambergate-Buxton branch. This involved boring the 1¾-mile Dove Holes tunnel through the Peak Forest hills.

The LNWR retaliated against the Midland's invasion of London by extending its influence in Cumbria. Here the Midland's traffic for Carlisle over the Clapham-Ingleton branch of the Settle/Lancaster/Morecambe line had to use the LNWR's main line over Shap. The Midland did not want to build its own route over those fells, which would have been an extremely expensive operation. The LNWR deliberately prolonged difficulties over joint operation between Ingleton and Carlisle and in 1866 the Midland embarked on its own Settle & Carlisle line. This is without doubt the wildest and grandest trunk route in Britain, with long, tough gradients, 19 viaducts and more than three miles of tunnels. After completing this line in 1876 the Midland opened its through service from London to Scotland, operating in conjunction with the Glasgow & South Western to Glasgow, and the North British to Edinburgh.

In the west of Scotland generally the Caledonian and Glasgow & South Western systems intertwined. In some areas they worked harmoniously together but in others less peacefully, particularly on the Clyde coast, where they competed fiercely for traffic. The Caledonian operated the Glasgow, Narrhead and Kilmarnock line jointly with the G&SWR, although the route helped the rival Anglo-Scottish service. A similar partnership covered the exit from Glasgow to Paisley. The two companies also shared a Glasgow terminus at Bridge Street until 1879, when the G&SWR opened St Enoch station and the Caledonian moved to Glasgow Central.

In eastern Scotland the completion of the Forth Bridge in 1890 established the North British Railway as another trunk system. The bridge was made accessible to both Edinburgh and Glasgow traffic by means of a triangular junction built into the inter-city line. North of the river a more direct route from Edinburgh to Perth was opened in 1883 and Kinnaber Junction and Aberdeen were reached with the grant of running powers over the Caledonian's tracks approaching that city.

For about 20 years, from the mid-1840s, Aberdeen had been regarded as the future gateway for railways penetrating the Highlands. In fact the route built north of Perth across the Grampian mountains to Inverness via Forres in 1863 became the Highland Railway in 1865. A line was extended further northwards to Dingwall and Skye in 1870 and the main route opened to Wick and Thurso in 1874. The Skye line was extended to Kyle of Lochalsh in 1897 and in 1898 the Highland Railway opened the direct route from Aviemore to Inverness. Between Aviemore and Blair Atholl the British Rail system reaches its highest main line point at 1484ft on the summit at Druimuachdar.

The Scottish railway system was rounded off by the acquisition in 1870 by the Caledonian of a company which was building north-westward from Callander. Eventually the line twisted and climbed its way to Oban by way of the Pass of Brander after the Caledonian completed construction work, and when the route was opened in July 1880 it attracted considerable tourist traffic. Finally the spectacular West Highland line to Fort William was opened in August 1894, and was extended to Mallaig in 1901.

Railway expansion in the United Kingdom had virtually ceased by the beginning of the twentieth century and it was becoming evident that despite Parliamentary controls many areas of the country were already over-endowed with railways. The resulting multiplicity of separately owned stations, depots, yards and competing lines proved a major economic disadvantage, the effects of which have endured to the present day.

Passenger comfort in the closing decade of the Victorian era was one of extreme contrasts. It could still be an austere, trying and wearisome business or a matter of comparative luxury. Passengers were wise to set out with greatcoats and rugs and flasks. They were drawn along in bone-shaking four- or six-wheel carriages which were lit by smelly oil lamps but had no heating. There were no corridors and usually no toilet facilities. Usually journeys were not more than seven or eight hours long – except on Anglo-Scottish runs and those from London to the extreme South West – and these conditions seemed to have been mutely endured. However, an approach to better standards had begun in the 1870s when the Pullman Palace Car Company's superior coaches were introduced in Britain.

George Mortimer Pullman had formed the company in the United States in 1867 to build the higher grade of accommodation required for long-distance trains undertaking journeys of several

left:
Derby from the Midland Railway roundhouse in 1860. (National Railway Museum)

above:
A portrait of a guard in full dress on the Cambrian Railways. (Colourviews Picture Library)

days. In 1872 the General Manager of the Midland Railway, James Allport, visited the United States and recognised that the Pullmans might be a way of achieving the company's objective of offering better accommodation than its rivals. The Midland had that year taken the contentious step of providing third-class facilities on all its trains. Now a contract was drawn up for 18 Pullman cars to be shipped in parts to England and assembled at the Derby works. Day and night Pullman services were inaugurated between St Pancras and Bradford in 1874. The complete Pullman trains included second-class and third-class accommodation as well as parlour and sleeping cars for first-class passengers. Two years later the Midland's Anglo-Scottish express service included first-class Pullman drawing-room cars for day trains and sleepers on night runs. The Midland had made the astute move of re-classifying second-class travel as third-class and using second-class carriages as thirds. Thereafter all third-class passenger rolling stock was built to what had previously been

second-class standards, with padded seats and backs. At a time when other companies were still using rigid wheelbase six-wheeler coaches on expresses, Midland passengers on the Anglo-Scottish service rode in comfort in compartment coaches carried on bogies.

Strangely, it was these compartment coaches which, in the long term proved more popular than the first-class Pullmans with their armchair seating, lamp-lit tables, toilet facilities and centre gangway layout. Even so, the credit for a change of heart by other companies in their design of passenger accommodation must go to the Midland for its introduction of Pullmans and the standard of its own coach-building. Pullman cars were used by a few other companies, including sleepers on the East Coast route and day-time parlour cars on the London–Brighton service. They lasted longest on the short south coast journeys.

The first sleeping cars had been introduced in Britain shortly before Pullmans were imported; the Ashbury Railway Carriage and Iron Company built a six-wheel convertible for use on the East Coast route in 1873 and in the same year the LNWR introduced a sleeping car of its own design on the Euston–Glasgow service. The

Last days of Brunel's dream – scene at Teignmouth, south Devon, shows the down 'Cornishman' in May 1892, just prior to final gauge conversion. Note the short sleepers already cut and laid nearby. The locomotive is a small 'convertible' 2–4–0. (C J Allen collection)

right:
Bletchley station *circa* 1900. A Webb Compound 2–2–2 No 644 *Vesuvius* double-heads a Precedent class 2–4–0 on a long Cambridge train. Unfortunately the identity of neither engine is known. (Colourviews Picture Library)

The final trunk route to be built (and the first to go) was the Manchester, Sheffield & Lincolnshire's extension south to London (Marylebone via Leicester and Rugby). This picture shows an inaugural train running into Brackley station on the opening day, 9 March 1899. From then on the railway was named the Great Central. (Leicester Library)

The first two return tickets, London to Manchester and back, were issued at the then-new Marylebone station, 15 March 1899. (Colourviews Picture Library)

An LNWR 'Lady of the Lake' class 2–2–2 with a 15-coach train made up of eight-wheeled bogie and six-wheeled stock (about 1900) heads up the West Coast main line. The second and third vehicles carry destination boards. (Colourviews Picture Library)

left:
Great Eastern Railway up express on Ipswich troughs with rebuilt T19 2–4–0 No 1022 later rebuilt as a 4–4–0 in 1900. (C J Allen collection)

Pullman retained, for a time, the advantage of having its own built-in hot water heating system. The normal method of heating in lesser passenger coaches was the footwarmer, a type of hot water bottle which passengers hired at various stations. The low-pressure steam method of heating passenger rolling stock was not introduced until 1884 and it was another 20 years before nearly all trains were fitted.

In 1879 a kitchen was built into a Pullman car on the Great Northern. It was demonstrated on a run from London to Peterborough and then used regularly from November of that year for first-class passengers on the Leeds–Kings Cross service. It was the first regular railway dining car with meals cooked on board in Britain. Passengers using the service paid the full Pullman supplement. Although some coaches at this time had corridors there was still no communication between coaches and this restricted the use of a restaurant service. In 1891 the Great Eastern introduced a set of four six-wheeled coaches which had inter-connections. One coach of the set, which was used on the 'North Country Continental' from Harwich, was a first-class dining car while the third-class passengers, who were not admitted to this car, had a folding table on which meals were served from the kitchen in one coach only. It was the GWR which introduced the first non-Pullman corridor train with vestibule connections between the coaches on the London–Birkenhead service

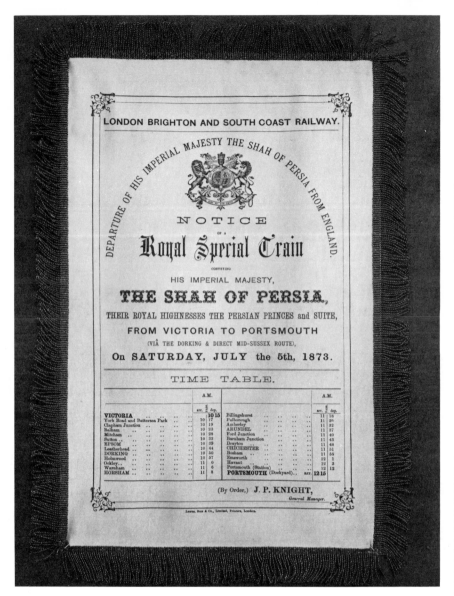

A Stirling of the South Eastern & Chatham Class F 4–4–0 heads a train of six wheelers somewhere in the London area around the turn of the century. Note the safety valves on top of the dome, the Westinghouse brake pump ahead of the leading driving wheel splasher and the outside springing of the small tender. (C J Allen collection)

The cover of the working timetable issued by the London Brighton & South Coast Railway in conjunction with the special train for the Shah of Persia, 5 July 1873. (P B Whitehouse collection)

One of Patrick Stirling's 4–2–2 express engines, built for the Great Northern Railway, was used in the famous 'Race to the North' against the West Coast companies. Relegated to more menial tasks in 1901, No 1004 is still spotlessly clean. (Colourviews Picture Library)

Midland and Great Northern Railway 4–4–0 No 55 with a train of six-wheeled stock in 1901. (Colourviews Picture Library)

in 1892. It did not have restaurant facilities. From 1893 East and West Coast companies introduced complete corridor restaurant-car trains available to all classes.

Despite some tentative experiments with gas lighting, oil lamps predominated into the early 1890s. Lighting by gas produced from oil was tested in an LNWR express in 1875 and first installed widely by the Metropolitan Railway in London in 1876. Experiments with electric lighting were carried out by the London, Brighton & South Coast Railway in 1881, using batteries in a single Pullman and then, in 1889, a dynamo on a four-car Pullman train. The dynamo was belt-driven from the axles and charged the batteries, thus being the forerunner of the standard system employing a dynamo under every coach.

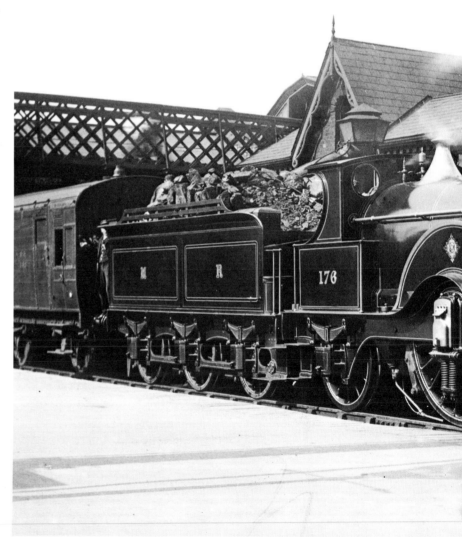

Though the steam train was the fastest means of transport in Victorian years, it was still not as fast as it could have been. Speeds were generally set below those which locomotives were capable of achieving because of the lack of sufficiently powerful brakes, problems of signal spacing, traffic density and the curvature of track – all of which had to be considered in planning timetables. There were two famous occasions when locomotives were pushed to their limits on the East and West Coast routes. These were in the so-called 'Railway Races' from London to Edinburgh in 1888 and to Aberdeen in 1895.

The announcement by the Great Northern in 1887 that it would admit third-class passengers to its daily morning expresses between London and Scotland, which at that time took nine hours to reach Edinburgh, was the spur which brought about the first of the races.

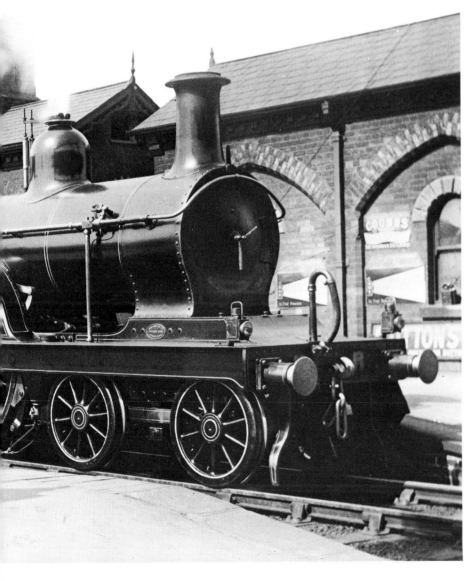

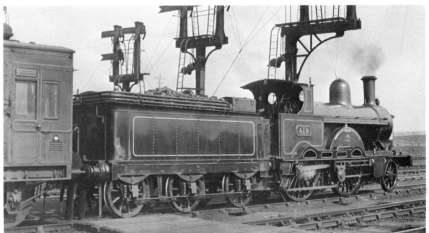

Towards the end of the nineteenth century F W Webb, the Chief Mechanical Engineer to the London & North Western Railway, built several experimental series of compound locomotives using two high- and one low-pressure cylinders. Shown here is No 519 *Shooting Star* at Chester with a local train around 1900, after being put out to grass by Webb's successor George Whale. (P B Whitehouse collection)

Caledonian Railway 4–4–0 No 729 (later LMS No 14319) of McIntosh's Dunalastair I class. (Cecil J Allen collection)

left:
The London & North
Western Railway 2–4–0
No 790 *Hardwicke* is now
preserved in the National
Railway Museum, York.
This famous engine
participated in the 'Race to
the North' in 1895. (C M
Whitehouse)

GREAT NORTHERN RAILWAY COMPANY'S HOTELS
ADJOIN THE STATIONS AT
KING'S CROSS GR GR & LEEDS
PETERBORO BRADFORD
PORTERS MEET ALL TRAINS AND CONVEY VISITORS' LUGGAGE TO THE HOTELS FREE
A SPACIOUS DINING ROOM IS PROVIDED ON THE DEPARTURE PLATFORM AT KING'S CROSS

This notice advertising the
Great Northern Railway
Company's hotels would
have been affixed to a panel
above the seats to ensure that
passengers were fully aware
of the services offered.
(Colourviews Picture
Library)

below:
This Highland Railway
Jones Goods class 4–6–0
No 103 is now preserved.
(P B Whitehouse)

above:
Three of these ancient London & South Western Railway Beattie 2–4–0 tanks were kept specially for service over the Wenford Bridge mineral branch in Cornwall. Here is the daily goods train at Helland behind No 30585 as late as September 1959. (Derek Cross)

Southern Railway No W3 *Carisbrooke* was sold by the LBSCR to the Isle of Wight Railway and taken over at Grouping thus rejoining the fold. (H C Casserley)

The West Coast expresses from Euston already took third-class passengers but the journey took ten hours. Accordingly the partners involved in this route replied in the summer of 1888 with the announcement that from 2 June the morning express from Euston would also cover the Edinburgh run in nine hours. A series of leap-frogging moves continued throughout that summer until 13 August, when the East Coast companies scheduled their Kings Cross express to reach Edinburgh in just 7 hours 45 minutes. The first train on this new schedule was late but on the same day the Euston train reached Edinburgh in 7 hours 38 minutes. The East Coast made the run in 7 hours 32 minutes the next day. Such timings were, in fact, impractical for regular operation and thereafter by mutual consent the East Coast set a time of 8 hours 15 minutes and the West Coast 8 hours 30 minutes, the latter's route being $7\frac{3}{4}$ miles longer.

When the Forth Bridge was opened in 1890 it made the route between Kings Cross to Aberdeen 16 miles shorter than that from Euston. The East Coast companies set out to exploit this advantage when the Highlands began to attract an increasing tourist traffic. Thus in the summer of 1895 another 'race' was joined between the two rival partnerships. The two overnight express routes converged at Kinnaber Junction, 38 miles south of Aberdeen and from there the East Coast train ran over the line of the Caledonian, a member of the West Coast partnership. On one occasion, when the contest was at its height, the signalman at Kinnaber Junction, who was employed by the Caledonian, was offered both the expresses at the same time. Sportingly, he gave the road to the East Coast rival, which reached Aberdeen from Kings Cross in 8 hours 40 minutes – two minutes longer than the best East Coast time, achieved on 22 August. On that day the West Coast train completed its run in 8 hours 32 minutes for an overall average speed of more than 60mph, despite stops at Crewe, Carlisle, Stirling and Perth. The highest start-to-stop average speed of 67.2mph was achieved on the Preston to Carlisle section, over Shap, by the 2–4–0 *Hardwicke*.

Although train weights were reduced to uneconomic levels for these special efforts, the performances achieved were remarkable for the time. By the end of the first 50 years of Britain's railways the average train speed for passenger expresses was just over 40mph, allowing for intermediate stops. That average was substantially above performances elsewhere and even in countries such as the United States and in Europe it was not equalled until after the turn of the century.

The key to higher speed was better braking. Early locomotive designers were unwilling to fit brakes directly to engines and even as late as the 1870s many passenger trains ran with brakes on tenders and brake vans at the front and back of the train. Guards worked the brakes by hand, obeying whistle signals from the drivers.

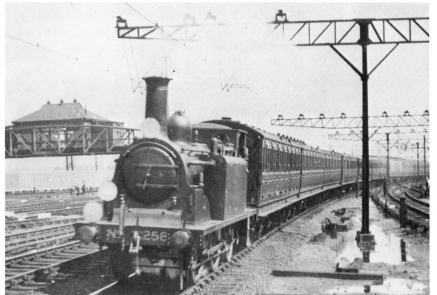

The traffic into Waterloo, Charing Cross and Victoria at peak commuting periods has always been extremely dense. Electrification was the obvious answer to quick turnround and rapid acceleration. This picture shows an LBSCR tank with a heavy train of close-coupled stock passing under the Brighton line's overhead electrified wires about 1920 but the train is pure Edwardian. (H C Casserley)

above:
Vital bridge: The building of the Forth and Tay bridges considerably shortened the East Coast partners route to Aberdeen. The grandeur of the great cantilevers of the Forth Bridge still appeals today when the smokestains have been weathered away from the approach arches. (Colourviews Picture Library)

Because of its nearness to the open road between Wisbech and Upwell in East Anglia, this Great Eastern Railway 0–6–0 No 127 was fitted with skirts and was 'boxed in' to avoid frightening the local livestock. This unusual standard gauge tramway continued to work freight until after World War II. (Colourviews Picture Library)

far left:
The Highland Railway around the turn of the century. This painting by J D Goffey shows one of the celebrated *Skye Bogie* 4–4–0s No 85 at Kyle of Lochalsh. (Colourviews Picture Library)

left:
Oban station in Edwardian days (from a painting by F Moore) shows the magnificent livery of the Caledonian Railway's locomotives. (Colourviews Picture Library)

London Brighton and South
Coast Railway's 4–4–0
No 64 *Norfolk* heads a
Brighton express in the livery
of umber brown which the
company adopted in 1905.
(Colourviews Picture Library)

below left:
Midland Railway single
wheeler No 118 (now
preserved) shows clearly the
find standard of painting
with the company's earlier
diamond-shaped coat of arms
on the splasher. (John Adams)

After witnessing an appalling train crash, the American George Westinghouse started work to improve braking and he patented the continuous compressed-air brake system in 1873. Its essential features were that the brakes could be applied throughout the train by the driver and that if the train parted while on the move the brakes on both sections were automatically applied. Though the system was eventually adopted by some British companies, most chose instead the continuous vacuum brake – a simpler and cheaper but less powerful and slower-acting alternative. This later proved a major technical handicap in the modernisation of stock by British Railways.

Back in the 1870s and 1880s most companies were reluctant to adopt continuous braking because it involved the expensive business of fitting brakes to all vehicles. When they did adopt the system it was generally fitted only to passenger vehicles. However, after a

An example of Great Western Railway dual gauge track. All 7′ 0″ gauge running ceased as from 1892. (British Rail/Oxford Publishing Co.)

As traffic increased steadily on Britain's railways, locomotives capable of hauling the increased loads became in short supply. The Midland attempted to overcome this problem by purchasing 'kits' from the Baldwin Locomotive Works in the USA. Assembly was at Derby works where this photograph was taken about 1900. (Colourviews Picture Library)

right:
A Midland Railway Baldwin 2–6–0 as station pilot at New Street, Birmingham. (Colourviews Picture Library)

catastrophe at Armagh in 1889 when 78 people were killed in an accident which could have been prevented by continuous braking and the block section signal system with the electric telegraph, Parliament made the installation of both mandatory.

The end of the broad gauge on the GWR had become accepted by the 1870s and some of the company's goods tank engines built in 1872 were constructed so that they could be converted to standard gauge. In addition broad gauge locomotive design was allowed to stagnate for more than 30 years, up to the GWR's eventual conversion to standard gauge in 1892. In the meantime the standard-gauge

North Eastern Railway class Z1 Atlantic 728 heads the 2.20 pm Edinburgh–Kings Cross away from Newcastle past Gateshead. From a painting by F Moore. (Colourviews Picture Library)

right:
H A Ivatt's Great Northern Railway 4–4–2 Atlantic No 280 leaves the south entrance of Hadley Wood tunnel with an up express during Edwardian days. From a painting by F Moore. (E S Russell collection)

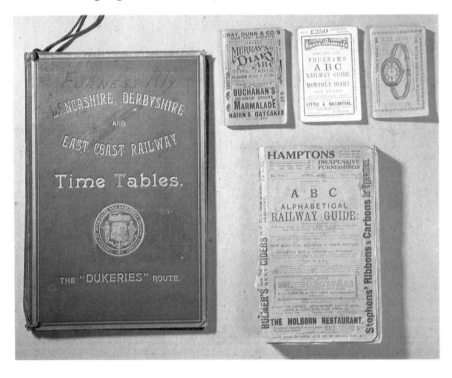

far left:
A rare example of the Lancashire, Derbyshire & East Coast Railway timetable plus examples of the many ABC types of table available throughout the country. (P B Whitehouse collection)

left:
Robert H Whitelegg's massive 4–6–4T of the Glasgow & South Western Railway heads a Stranraer-to-Glasgow (St Enoch) boat express near Ibrox in 1922. By D Goffey. (Colourviews Picture Library)

railways were producing locomotives capable of matching the performance of those of the GWR.

During the 1870s the majority of British express passenger engines were of 2–2–2, 4–2–2, 2–4–0 or 4–4–0 configurations. With the standard of track greatly improved so that the steel lines were strong and firm, the six-wheeled engines were performing safely and well at high speeds. There were some notable performers among the 2–4–0s, of which the Kirtley 800 class of the Midland and the 901 class of the North Eastern were outstanding. But the first standard-gauge engines really to rival the GWR's broad-gauge types were the Stirling 4–2–2s. These had 8ft diameter driving wheels and outside

cylinders and were built for the Great Northern from 1870 onwards. The famous Stirling single No 1 is preserved as part of the national railway collection. Earlier Stirling engines were six-wheelers with inside cylinders; Stirling made the change to lower the boiler and improve stability and incidentally produced a locomotive with considerably more graceful lines than most contemporaries. The stability of the Stirling design was underlined in the slightly later 2–2–2s with 7ft 6in driving wheels and inside cylinders. The two types were used on similar duties with little difference in performance. The Stirling singles continued to be built until 1893–94 and it was amply proved that, in favourable conditions, engines with single driving axles performed well. Less power was absorbed in the drive

than was the case in coupled engines of the same size, so more was available at the drawbar. However, under conditions that made the driving wheels slip, such as a sudden rainstorm, the pulling power of the engine was frequently reduced. Many companies came to consider the 2–4–0 and 4–4–0 as more suitable for everyday work, despite the improvement in tractive ability brought about by the Holt sand blast in the mid-1880s. This used steam or compressed air to blow sand under the driving wheels to provide a better grip on the rails.

The Midland had a very similar experience to the Great Northern with its Johnson inside-cylinder 4–2–2s with drivers of up to 7ft 4in. The first of several batches of these appeared in 1884. Alongside

Great Eastern Railway 0–8–0
– the rebuild of the unwanted
Decapod. (C J Allen
collection)

Britain's first 4–6–0,
Highland Railway No 103,
leaves the Kyle of Lochalsh
with the early morning
mixed train for Dingwall.
This engine, restored to the
Highland livery, was
running in regular service for
the BBC TV series Railway
Roundabout in 1960.
(P B Whitehouse)

A Waterloo–Bournemouth express passes Beaulieu Road station on the London & South Western Railway. The locomotive is one of Drummond's 'Paddlebox' 4–6–0s. (C Hamilton Ellis courtesy Viscount Garnock)

BEAULIEU ROAD

similarly powered Johnson 4–4–0s, the difference in performance was not significant; the singles were occasionally outstanding and it was generally thought that they were lighter on coal but the coupled engines were more reliable in bad weather. Several classes of Webb engines on the LNWR were intended to combine the good qualities of single and coupled drive by having two separate (that is, un-coupled) driving axles driven by separate cylinders. On simple-expansion four cylinder engines the results were indifferent but on three-cylinder compound classes, good performance and fuel economy were achieved, though not necessarily only – or even mainly – because of the uncoupled four-wheel drive.

Performance capability of Caledonian Railway passenger locomotives was advanced considerably in 1896 with the introduction of the McIntosh Dunalastair class, which was little more than a standard 4–4–0 design fitted with a bigger boiler. The favourable results with the Dunalastair induced other designers to adopt large boilers. Wilson Wordsell's class R 4–4–0 was in service on the North Eastern just before the turn of the century and the Johnson 4–4–0s with Belpaire boilers of the Midland, and Claud Hamiltons of the Great Eastern appeared early in 1900. The large boiler 4–4–0 was thus set to play a major role on early twentieth century expresses.

An even bigger locomotive to replace the Stirling singles was being planned by H A Ivatt. In the United States the 4–4–2 Atlantic type was gaining a good reputation for high-speed running and Ivatt built Britain's first Atlantic type in 1888. It was No 990 *Henry Oakley*, which is preserved in the National Railway Museum. This, his first 4–4–2 design, had a narrow firebox but he followed with a larger boilered Atlantic design which had a wide firebox more akin to the American originals.

Several railways adopted the Atlantic as the logical successor to the 4–2–2 for passenger express work but as train loads increased, the tendency for the driving wheels to slip on wet rails became a problem. The answer came eventually in the use of three coupled axles on the 4–6–0s and 4–6–2 Pacific types, but they did not become common as heavy passenger express engines until well into the twentieth century.

The steam locomotive had made great progress in the second half of the nineteenth century. The GWR's broad-gauge 4–2–2 of 1847 had been brilliant and well ahead of contemporary design but the standard-gauge Dunalastair of 1896, with much the same size of boiler and grate, could haul trains of twice the weight at comparable speeds.

While trains had become the accepted means of long-distance

above:
George Jackson Church-ward's four-cylinder 4–6–0 Star class of the GWR when new in 1910. Note the 3500-gallon tender. The coaches were then in red/brown livery. The locomotive is No 4035 *Queen Charlotte*. (Cecil J Allen collection)

A Great Western double-framed 0–6–0 takes a train of six-wheelers on the main line from Birmingham to Leamington. (H W Burman –P B Whitehouse collection)

travel, they also served for short journeys in towns and cities. New suburbs began to be built beyond centuries-old city boundaries and by the mid-Victorian era workers were no longer living within walking distance of their places of employment. Clerks and artisans and workmen moved out from the centres either into the country or to the edge of the towns where they worked. Some railways

A North Eastern Railway
composite clerestory coach
used for push-pull working
around the turn of the
century. The locomotive is
an 0–4–4 well tank of
Class BTP. (Colourviews
Picture Library)

Contemporary painting of troops entraining for the Boer War. The destination board on the brake van says Southampton and the coach colours are those of the LSWR. (Colourviews Picture Library)

suburban services into Manchester and senior administrators in the shipping and textile industries travelled from as far as the Lake District and the North Wales coast. They sometimes used first-class-only trains which included club saloons admitting members only. Around Glasgow the Caledonian, the Glasgow & South Western and the North British fought for commuter traffic from the Clyde coast dormitory towns.

The in-town suburban trains continued to have non-corridor compartment coaches – often four-wheeled until World War I – hauled by tank engines which were usually small 0–6–0Ts, 0–4–4Ts or 0–4–2Ts. These were supplemented in the first decade of the twentieth century by larger 0–6–2Ts, or 4–4–2Ts or even larger engines on longer-distance services. On these longer-distance commuter trains corridor coaches were introduced earlier as the commuting habit placed people further from their work.

around London, particularly the North London, Great Eastern and London, Brighton & South Coast, encouraged the resulting commuter traffic with frequent trains and cheap workmen's fares, though the fare levels, as we have seen, were sometimes imposed by Parliament.

By the early 1900s members of the management echelons commuted daily between the Surrey hills or even the South coast and London. A similar pattern emerged around large provincial cities. The Lancashire & Yorkshire Railway, in particular, ran intensive

The London Brighton and South Coast Railway 0–4–2 *Gladstone* complete with Royal train headlamps and coat of arms in the National Railway Museum at York. (Eric Treacy)

Racers at York: London & North Western Railway 2–4–0 No 890 *Hardwicke* faces North Eastern Railway 2–4–0 No 910 heading a Great Northern coach at York station. These engines representing the great Race to Aberdeen of 1895 are now in the National Railway Museum. (Colourviews Picture Library/P Harris)

A member of one of the
finest classes of 4–4–0 to be
built, the London & North
Western Railway's George
the Fifth Class aptly named
Fire Queen, takes an express
out of Euston. (C Hamilton
Ellis)

3

GROUPING AND NATIONALISATION

FOUR MAIN LINES

The railways of Britain reached their peak in the two decades after the introduction of corridor trains to the outbreak of World War I in 1914. Speeds were higher than before, trains heavier and locomotives more powerful to cope with their extra loads. Electric lighting and steam heating were becoming standard equipment and the internal decor of passenger vehicles was elaborate. Express trains of the period were probably in their most elegant period.

Even so, the first signs of changing conditions which would result in the decline of railways were already appearing. Though the advent of the internal combustion engine towards the end of the nineteenth century did not attract much public attention, by the turn of the century motor vehicles on the roads were becoming a practical proposition. In addition, and more seriously, the development of the electric motor as a means of generating and distributing power had opened the way for electric trams to challenge urban railways for their passenger traffic. In a small way the railways began to use electric power, too, but not yet to any great extent.

Overshadowing all was the growing threat of war which eventually broke in August 1914. The next four years were to impose severe strains on the country's railway system. However, in anticipation of war a Railway Executive Committee was set up in 1912. It consisted of railway general managers and was charged with running the railways as a single co-ordinated system if the need arose. When that need did arise in 1914 the scheme worked well and in only 16 days the railways carried thousands of men, horses and guns of the British Expeditionary Force to Southampton to cross to France. Similarly, plans existed, when war was declared, for the conversion of railway rolling stock to form ambulance trains and by the end of the month 12 such trains were ready.

The Railway Executive Committee controlled 130 railway companies or joint committees and 21,331 route miles. The total railway work force was about 60,000 but more than 30 per cent of employees joined the forces. Shortage of railway staff was by no means the only problem; for example the Highland Railway in particular was overtaxed by the heavy traffic it had to carry for provisioning the

Grand Fleet at Scapa Flow. The Executive arranged for it to borrow locomotives from other companies and to have its own engines repaired by outside contractors. In addition the company's locomotive, carriage and wagon superintendent prepared designs for a new 4–6–0 which was to be known as the River class. Sadly, when the first of the six in the class was delivered it was found that its axle-load was too high; the locomotives were useless on that company's lines and were sold to the Caledonian.

Efforts were made during the war to discourage civilian travel, though with little effect, but passenger services were restricted. Even the draconian measures taken in 1917 of abolishing cheap fares and increasing ordinary fares by 50 per cent, with further drastic cuts in services had relatively little effect.

An ex-London & North Western Railway Claughton class 4–6–0 takes water at Bushey heading a 13-coach train. The locomotive is still in LNWR black with its company's cast numberplate and the leading coach is also in its maker's livery of plum and spilt milk. The date of the photograph is about 1926, just after Grouping. (John Adams)

After the Armistice of 11 November 1918 the Government continued outright control of the railways until 15 August 1921. Then the Railways Act set out the framework for the wholesale amalgamations of railway companies which became known as the 'Grouping'. In fact, demands for railway nationalisation to consolidate the various useful wartime measures of standardisation and rationalisation under a central body were widespread. However, all-out nationalisation was rejected in favour of the 1921 Act under which 120 railway companies were to be reorganised into four groups from 1 January 1923. The plans for 'Grouping' had been drawn up without any consultation with the companies and various anomalies, such as penetrations by some groups into the territories of others, were enshrined in the Act to the detriment of harmony and full efficiency.

Eight constituents went to make up the largest of the new groups, the London Midland & Scottish Railway (LMS): the London & North Western, the Midland, the Lancashire & Yorkshire, the North Staffordshire, the Caledonian, the Furness, the Glasgow & South Western and the Highland Railways. With 27 subsidiaries, the group had 7500 route miles. The London & North Western and the Lancashire & Yorkshire had worked closely together for years and anticipated the Grouping by amalgamating in January 1922. The LNWR and the Midland also bequeathed to the LMS the Northern Counties Committee and the Dundalk, Newry & Greenore Railway.

In its early days the LMS was chronically short of express motive power and until the coming of the Royal Scots in 1927 ex-LNWR Claughtons and (as shown here) L & Y 4–6–0s often needed double-heading with anything like a heavy load. This photograph shows ex-LNWR Precursor class No 5263 piloting an unknown L & Y 4–6–0 out of Carlisle. (P B Whitehouse collection)

As the LMS had been formed from the companies along the West Coast route, so the London & North Eastern Railway group (LNER) came from the East Coast companies. It had seven constituents: the North Eastern, the Great Northern, Great Eastern, Great Central, Hull & Barnsley, North British and the Great North of Scotland. There were 26 subsidiaries and the group had a total mileage of about 6700. Among the companies, the North Eastern and the Hull & Barnsley had merged on 1 January 1922. The Great Central was something of a problem because of its cross-country main line in the north and its London main line; both encroached on LMS territory. But it eventually provided the LNER with a useful relief route between London and the North East.

The only line to remain largely intact was the Great Western, which retained its name and its previous structure. The seven constituents were the GWR itself and, in Wales, the Barry, Cambrian, Rhymney, Taff Valley, Cardiff and the Alexandra (Newport & South Wales) Docks & Railways. It also absorbed 26 subsidiary companies to provide a new route mileage for the GWR of 3800 miles.

The new Southern Railway was the smallest of the groups, with only about 2200 route miles. Its constituents were the London & South Western, the South Eastern, the London, Chatham & Dover

MAIN ROUTES
of the
LONDON & NORTH
EASTERN
RAILWAY

FORWARD

above:
A double framed GWR 4–4–0 of the *Bulldog* class takes a local train down the main line near Newnham in 1923. Note the typical flat arch bridge, the platelayer's hut made from sleepers, the clerestory coach, the eliptical roof six wheeler local train set and the wooden milk vans. (P B Whitehouse Collection)

The same spot showing a Churchward express freight 2–8–0 of the 47XX class with a down perishable goods train. Note that in both photographs the bars on the telegraph poles are on the far (London) side thus indicating direction. (P B Whitehouse Collection)

and the London, Brighton & South Coast. There were 14 subsidiaries. The SER and LCDR had formed the South Eastern & Chatham Railways Joint Managing Committee on 1 August 1899 to rationalise services and work the lines of both companies. That organisation continued until Grouping.

Although the Southern was small it made up for this with the density of its traffic in south-east England and the sprawling suburban areas of London south of the Thames. Various suburban electrification schemes, which had been in hand at the time of Grouping, were continued and the Southern eventually reached the coast with an electric system. The SECR and LB&SCR brought into the group the relatively short-distance Continental boat trains and the 'Southern Belle' all-Pullman London–Brighton express and the L&SW contributed its main lines to Bournemouth and to the West Country.

Perhaps inevitably, the enforced merging of so many companies brought problems to some of the new groups, though the change went quite smoothly for the Great Western, which was virtually unaffected. On the LMS rivalries between men from the constituent companies caused disruptions which lasted for a decade. The post of Chief Mechanical Engineer went to George Hughes, from the Lancashire & Yorkshire. Policy at the main centres, Crewe, Derby and St Rollox, on the Caledonian, was little changed until his retirement in 1925. Then Sir Henry Fowler, who had been Chief Mechanical Engineer at Derby, took over and immediately began a programme to standardise LMS locomotives. This resulted in a predominance of smaller engines because as older locomotives were made redundant they were replaced with new engines from what were considered the best of the remaining designs. These tended to be from the former Midland Railway, which had favoured small engines. As a result, the LMS operators on the West Coast route, which required large locomotives, felt they were being neglected.

Eventually the LMS ran short of locomotives powerful enough to haul the increasing weight of trains. The need for a new six-coupled design could not be overlooked. In 1926 a Castle class 4–6–0 had been borrowed from the GWR and had performed excellently. An LMS 4–6–0 was quickly designed and the North British Locomotive Company Limited received an order to build 50 of the three-cylinder Royal Scots, as the class was named. In fact, the class performed well and proved themselves more than a mere stop-gap until W A (later Sir William) Stanier was appointed CME in 1932 and began a new era of locomotive design.

The 4–4–0 had been the established express locomotive at the turn of the century, 4–4–2s were being introduced on some lines and the 4–6–0 had just appeared in a few designs of goods or small mixed-traffic engines. However, the 4–6–0 concept was expanded to much

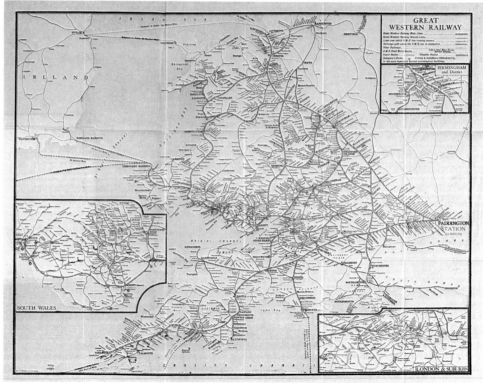

Although originally built for the Highland Railway the River Class 4–6–0s were sold to the Caledonian due to weight problems. In this painting, representing the early days of the LMS at Aviemore, No 14759 has at last come to the Highlands with a southbound Inverness–Perth passenger train. From a painting by C. Hamilton Ellis. (Colourviews Picture Library)

GWR 0–6–0 No 2541 shunts at Kinnersley yard on the daily pick-up from Hereford to Brecon. (P M Alexander)

below:
A Great North of Scotland 0–4–2T as LNER No 8191 shunts fish vans at Aberdeen harbour in 1947. (H C Casserley)

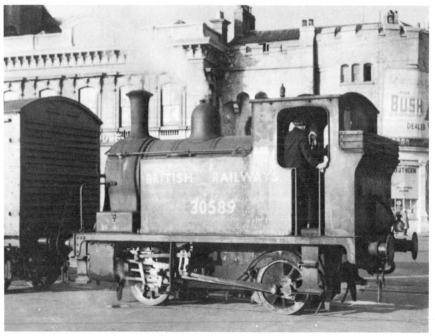

An unusual engine – in the form of an ex-LSWR railcar unit – 0–4–0T No 30589 runs down the road at Southampton docks in 1949. (P M Alexander)

larger proportions by J F McIntosh of the Caledonian in 1903 when he built two, No 49 and No 50, which were essentially Dunalastair 4–4–0s expanded into six-couplers. These, which were claimed as Britain's largest and most powerful express locomotives, were overtaken by McIntosh's larger version, the 903 or *Cardean* class. The engine which gave its name to the class, No 903 *Cardean*, worked almost daily on the afternoon express from Glasgow to Euston, running as far as Carlisle and returning on the 'down' express. In 1909 *Cardean* achieved unexpected fame when being tested over the LNWR line between Carlisle and Preston. Running fully extended uphill with a load of 390 tons, it sustained a speed of 44mph up the 1-in-75 gradient of Shap.

Though the early six-coupled engines were much publicised, there was, in truth, little room for further development of the saturated steam engine for express passenger work. When fully extended such an engine was burning coal so fast that it was not only uneconomic but also unreasonable to expect the fireman to sustain the stoking rate. The problem of how to reduce coal consumption had concerned some designers at least since the mid-1880s. On the LNWR Francis Webb had experimented with compounds, hoping that the 're-cycling' of steam was the answer but he had only limited success. His successor, George Whale, replaced the compounds with engines of great simplicity, the most successful being the Precursor class 4–4–0.

The relative scarcity and expensiveness of coal in France had provided the incentive for more intensive work on perfecting the compound. One of the outstanding results was the De Glehn compound Atlantic class which put up magnificent performances on the Nord Railway and also attracted the attention of British designers. One of them was G J Churchward, of the Great Western, who, after looking at the best locomotives of the world, aimed to design one which made use of all their best features. He wanted at least to match the theoretical efficiency of a compound cylinder arrangement by improving the steam expansion ration in simple-cylinder locomotives. To achieve this he used long-lap, long-travel valves (instead of the traditional short-lap, short-travel valves of saturated steam engines). In addition he solved the problem of steam leakage past pistons and valves and perfected a correctly proportioned boiler. He carried out tests on GWR tracks with a four-cylinder Nord-type compound Atlantic and two 4–4–2s of the type used on the Paris–Orleans run. He tested them all against his own two-cylinder simple 4–4–2s and 4–6–0s. All the locomotives exceeded Churchward's aim of a draw-

Thomas Cook devised one of the earliest railway excursions and these were a regular part of the railway scene during the days of the private companies. This LNER train, double headed by a North Eastern 4–4–0 and a B16 class 4–6–0 is about to leave Leyburn for London with a special to view the Solar eclipse on 26 June 1927. (H C Casserley)

The Southern Railway inherited the 2ft 0in gauge Lynton & Barnstaple Railway in 1923. Never an economic reality the section was closed in 1935. Here is the American-built Baldwin tank No 762 Lyn leaving Barnstaple in 1934. (D. E. H. Box)

In steam days the use of pusher or banker engines to assist the train engine when climbing steep inclines was more frequent than it is with diesel traction. This was particularly the case with heavy freight trains. Three LMS engines No 7638, No 7308 and No 3433 help a heavy freight to ascend the Lickey incline from Bromsgrove. (H C Casserley)

One of the very few narrow gauge systems to be incorporated into the 1923 grouping was the 2′ 0″ gauge Lynton & Barnstaple Railway. This delightful little byway lasted until 1935 and the painting by J. E. Hoyland shows the 2–6–2T *Exe* with a train near Barnstaple. (P B Whitehouse collection)

left:
One of the paintings specially commissioned by the LMS in the 1930s. Their intended attraction was that they were by members of the Royal Academy. (Colourviews Picture Library)

bar pull of two tons at 70mph and the British 4–6–0s proved as fast as the French Atlantics. However, the French compounds provided smoother riding than the 4–6–0s since they had better balancing and four cylinders compared with two outside cylinders taking powerful thrusts from 30-inch piston strokes.

As a result of his experiments Churchward built a four-cylinder Atlantic, *North Star*, which was followed by ten four-cylinder 4–6–0s. Thereafter he built further four-cylinder 4–6–0s, which took over much of the heavy work on West Country main lines. From the name of that first experimental four-cylinder engine the various types which followed were given the class name Star while his two-cylinder engines were classed as Saints.

British designers had come to appreciate in the early 1900s that the

efficiency of their locomotives was improved either by compounding or by building on the Churchward principle of simple, rationally designed locomotives. Even so, several large 4–6–0s designs had appeared which related to neither solution. These included the large and impressive Sir Sam Fay class on the GCR, the Drummond Paddleboxes on the LSWR and the Hughes four-cylinder 4–6–0s of the L&YR, none of which showed any significant advantages over smaller four-coupled types.

It was a German invention which provided the answer for British designers: the superheating system of Dr Wilhelm Schmidt. Incoming steam was divided to pass through a number of small tubes inserted into a suitably enlarged flue tube in the boiler. Steam could thus be dried and condensation reduced, with the result that a superheated engine used about 25 per cent less coal and water to produce the same performance as a saturated steam engine of the same class. Some classes were transformed by the installation of superheating and gave much superior performances.

Perhaps because his engines were already good, the improvement which superheating gave to Churchward's engines was more modest and he used a moderate superheating system instead of a high temperature one. On the other hand the LNWR went for full, high-temperature superheating and C J Bowen Cooke built a superheated Precursor 4–4–0 in 1910 which was named *George the Fifth*. Thanks to advice from Dr Schmidt, the valve design on this locomotive was bettered only on the GWR and the engine proved to have an almost insatiable appetite for hard work out of all proportion to its size.

Engines of the subsequent *George the Fifth* class regularly hauled trains of 400 tons and more at start-to-stop speeds of 55mph south of Preston and needed no assistance to take loads of up to 400 tons over Shap. Even so, the LNWR introduced express 4–6–0s, culminating in the Claughton class, which was intended to rival the Churchward Stars.

The next step from the 4–6–0 was the 4–6–2 Pacific type. The GWR was the first in the field in Britain with its four-cylinder experimental giant No 111 *The Great Bear*, built at Swindon in 1908. Though this famous engine pointed the way to the future, it was really ahead of its time and because the engineers restricted it to the Paddington–Bristol main line, it never proved itself more useful than either the Star or Saint class of 4–6–0s. Pacifics were not taken seriously until the 1920s. Then, just before Grouping, Nigel Gresley of the GNR built two for express service and Sir Vincent Raven followed with a Pacific for the NER. All were three-cylinder 4–6–2s

Although actually a 1980 scene, this picture, taken on the Severn Valley Railway at Bewdley, shows a typical Great Western scene of the 1930s. (P J. Howard)

left:
A 1938 photograph of a Stanier Duchess Pacific with its original single chimney and without smoke deflectors. No 6224 *Princess Alexandra* stands at Shrewsbury with a running in-turn from Crewe. (P B Whitehouse)

right:
The footplate of the record breaking LNER Class A4 Pacific No 4468 *Mallard*. (Colourviews Picture Library)

Double headed Castles with a
West of England train near
Thingley Junction,
Wiltshire. (P M Alexander)

and were intended as prototypes for new classes. When Gresley was appointed CME of the LNER he naturally picked his own Pacific.

The Great Western had claimed that *The Great Bear* was 'Britain's largest and most powerful passenger locomotive' and even in 1923, after Gresley's Pacific had appeared, they continued with the claim – this time applying it to the new four-cylinder 4–6–0 *Caerphilly Castle*, which was the first of a long and distinguished line of Castle class engines. The GWR's claim was based on the qualification of *theoretical* tractive effort but the LNER objected, saying that the true criterion of power was boiler size.

In 1924 a GWR Castle and an LNER Pacific were exhibited side by side at the Wembley exhibition and in the following year exchange trials were arranged between the two companies. These proved that the smaller GWR engine did its work on less coal not only on its 'home' lines but also on those of the LNER. Its performance was largely the result of its higher boiler pressure and better valve arrangement, which made the Castles more free-running and economical. The valve gear later became standard for many other locomotive types. Gresley also experimented by increasing boiler pressure from 180lb/sq in to 220 and this was adopted for all new Pacifics. One of these, class A3 No 2750 *Papyrus*, reached a maximum speed of 108mph in trials in 1935.

Henry Fowler designed the Royal Scot 4–6–0 for the LMS and from 1927 until the advent of Stanier in 1932, these were the principal express engines for that system. Later, when fitted with Stanier's taper boiler, their performance was revolutionised, but in 1939 No 6126 was as built and is seen here taking a Liverpool to London train past Edge Hill locomotive depot. (Eric Treacy)

An experimental turbine locomotive, the Swedish Ljungstrom locomotive carries express-train headlamps near Elstree on the ex-Midland main line. (P B Whitehouse collection)

Claims and counter-claims about the performance of the loco-motives of rival groups marked the year 1927 as one of keen com-petition. Towards the end of 1926 the Southern Railway had built a large four-cylinder 4–6–0, No 850 *Lord Nelson*, which had a tractive effort greater than that of a Castle. The Southern, using the GWR's formula, therefore claimed it had the most powerful passenger locomotive in Britain. It is doubtful if an engine of the class could have beaten a Castle in actual performance at that time. In the summer the GWR replied with an engine which carried the 4–6–0 arrange-ment to its greatest size in Britain: No 6000 *King George V*. This had a tractive effort of more than 40,000lb and the GWR promptly claimed it as 'Britain's mightiest passenger locomotive'. Subsequently the 30 King class engines gave excellent service, almost to the end of steam and *King George V* became one of the country's most famous locomotives.

Famous Crossing: A Gresley LNER Pacific No 2570 *Tranquil* leaves Newcastle Central station for the north over a complex crossing of tracks *circa* 1927. Note the electro-pneumatically controlled signal gantry. (National Railway Museum)

The King of Railway Locomotives – or so said the GWR publicity people. An unknown GWR King class 4–6–0 on Rowington water troughs north of Warwick in 1933. The taking of water at high speed from troughs between the tracks sometimes provided this Niagara Falls effect on the first coach of a train. (P B Whitehouse collection)

An LNER manually-operated signal box on the East Coast main line. Note the coloured levers, red for stop signals, yellow for distant signals and black for points. From the original painting by Terence Cuneo. (Courtesy British Railways)

A cross section of railway tickets including main line, light railways, special excursions and platform tickets. (Colourviews Picture Library)

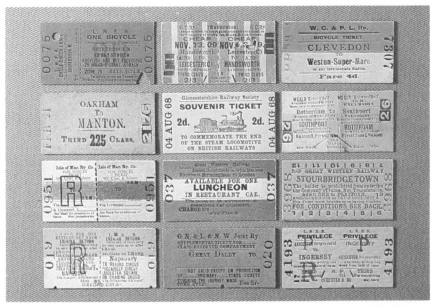

below:
GWR, LMS, Southern and LNWR booklets. (P B Whitehouse)

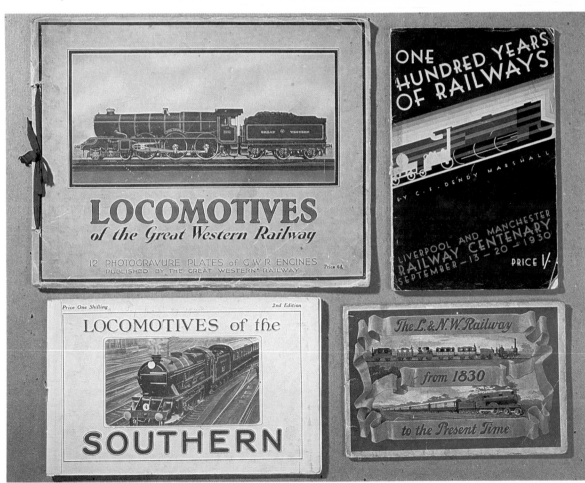

A selection of the Great Western Railway's books for 'Boys of All Ages'. (P B Whitehouse)

left:
An assortment of the excellent wooden jig-saw puzzles made by Chad Valley Ltd. for the GWR. (P B Whitehouse)

Stanier, whose appointment as CME of the LMS we have previously mentioned, joined the company from the Great Western, where he had been principal assistant to Churchward's successor, C B Collett. With the shortage of large locomotives to work the West Coast route in mind, Stanier designed No 6200 *The Princess Royal*, which was really a GWR King expanded into a Pacific. The engine was built in 1933 but the class did not achieve complete success until 1935, by which time they had been turned into powerful and efficient locomotives.

While most attention and publicity was centred on the design and performance of express passenger locomotives, it was the workhorses of the railways, the goods and mixed-traffic engines, which earned a large portion of the revenue. Fast goods and secondary passenger services were handled on the lines of all four groups in the 1920s by the 2–6–0 Moguls. However, in 1924 the GWR's 4–6–0 *Saint Martin* was rebuilt with driving wheels of 6ft 0in instead of 6ft 8in. This locomotive ushered in the modern mixed-traffic 4–6–0 type, the intention of the rebuilding being to increase pulling power at moderate speeds without detracting from possible maximum pace. Its success led to the building of the first of the GWR Hall class in 1928.

The LNER and LMS tried several experimental locomotive types in service. The Kitson-Still attempt to marry the steam engine to the internal combustion engine stands in the LNER York shed in 1933. (A W Flowers)

right:
The Great Western Railway absorbed the various independent lines in South Wales in the Grouping of 1923. A number of the more modern of the engines taken over were rebuilt at Swindon with taper boilers as was Taff Vale 0–6–2 (now GWR No 368) at Treherbert in 1938. (H C Casserley)

This class eventually totalled 330 engines which could be relied upon to complete virtually any task on the GWR.

In the 1930s William Stanier produced the first of his class 5 4–6–0s, the famous 'Black Fives', for the LMS. The class reached a total of 842 locomotives, a reliable measure of their success. After nationalisation in 1948 the Stanier design was used as the basis for the BR standard 73000 class of 172 engines.

Nigel Gresley, on the LNER, had different ideas about engine size and produced the very large 2–6–2s of the V2 or Green Arrow class. Able to handle the work of Pacifics, they carried out important duties hauling trains of up to 20 coaches in World War II. With an axle-load of 22 tons, they were restricted to main-line work but Gresley designed two smaller 2–6–2s, the Bantam Cock class, to handle secondary traffic. These sturdy engines could run almost anywhere. Shortly after they first had entered service Sir Nigel, as he then was, died. His successor was Edward Thompson, who preferred a two-cylinder 4–6–0 design, his LNER B1 class, which appeared in 1942. The class eventually numbered 410 and the engines gave a performance similar to that of the rival GWR and LMS 4–6–0s.

The majority of goods work was handled by 0–6–0s except for the very heavy duties, when 0–8–0s or 2–8–0s took over. Though the 'goods engine' reached its maximum size between the wars, maximum efficiency was not developed until the appearance of the standard BR 9F 2–10–0 in 1953.

Short-distance and suburban work was undertaken by the tank engines though at one time it seemed that these would also be used extensively on express work over medium-length journeys. Large express tank engines of the 4–6–4T Baltic type (really, self-contained 4–6–0s) were built by several companies but none proved particularly outstanding. The GWR used 2–6–2Ts for its local services and on other lines the 2–6–4T was employed on mixed traffic duties. After the derailment of a Southern Railway River class 2–6–4T at Sevenoaks in 1927 the type was mistrusted for a time but was later used extensively by the LMS, achieving maximum speeds of over 80mph.

An indication of the great improvement in engine design can be gained from the fact that between 1900 and 1939 the steam locomotive had doubled its maximum horsepower with only a 30 per cent increase in weight. It had also reduced its coal consumption per unit of work measured at the drawbar by about 40 per cent. Even so, it was still wasteful on fuel and high on maintenance costs. There were already rival forms of power threatening the dominance of the

steam locomotive: the GWR was using diesel railcars on some branch and cross-country services; the LMS had diesel shunting engines; and the Southern was pressing ahead with electrification.

After the end of World War I the railways took some time to return to the pre-war standards of express passenger train speeds. The exception was the Great Western, which seemed to have kept its engines well enough maintained to be able to restore 1914 timings on its principal routes from Paddington by 1921. But on most routes there were gaps in the timings between the fast trains and other services. Even after Grouping in 1923 standards remained erratic because locomotives had still not been restored to top condition after the war years of minimum maintenance and over-work. To boost the tarnished image, the railway companies sometimes selected a train for special treatment, naming it and improving its timings.

Though Anglo-Scottish timings remained, until the early 1930s, subject to the agreement reached after the 'great races' of 1888/95, the LMS and LNER still competed for glory in other ways. Long non-stop runs were the most effective form of competition and on 27 April 1928 the LMS stole the LNER's thunder by running the 'Royal Scot' train in two parts non-stop from Euston to Glasgow and

The GWR road service modernises. A *Karrier Cob* tractor attached to a horse dray, September 1931. (P B Whitehouse Collection)

The GWR also laid claim to run 'the fastest train in the world' when it raised the average speed between Swindon and Paddington to over 70mph of a lightweight and previously insignificant Cheltenham–London express, which became known as 'The Cheltenham Flyer'. There were moves elsewhere to capture new traffic and the LNER aimed at the luxury end of the market with new Pullman trains between Kings Cross and Yorkshire and with the 'Queen of Scots' to Glasgow. The Southern brought in new Pullman services for Bournemouth and for the 'Golden Arrow' between London and the Channel ports.

The railways were now also having to take steps to counter the growing competition from buses and motorcoaches which were able to link villages with urban centres, often at much lower fares. Fast cross-country and outer-suburban trains were introduced by the LNER. These included Kings Cross–Cambridge, Newcastle–Carlisle, Leeds–Scarborough and Hull–Liverpool. Buffet cars, which the LNER used widely on secondary services, were included in some of these trains.

Once again passenger accommodation came in for attention and improvement by the designers. In 1927 the LMS introduced a new type of coach which did away with compartment doors and was the forerunner of today's inter-city carriage. At first these were only used for first-class travel but by the start of the 1930s they were also built for third-class accommodation. First-class coaches for the 'Royal Scot' and other named expresses were laid out for just four

Edinburgh respectively three days before the LNER 'Flying Scotsman' began non-stop running between Kings Cross and Edinburgh. However, the LMS could not produce such runs to schedule whereas the 'Flying Scotsman' went on to claim and retain the world record for length of regular daily non-stop working.

Despite growing competition on the roads in the early 1930s, the train remained the most convenient means of travel and any national event was sure to attract and fill several excursion trains. In the summer the main-line routes to the coast were packed with so many extra trains that freight traffic and often local passenger services were curtailed. On Saturdays the GWR's 'Cornish Riviera' express, normally a single train, often had to run in as many as four parts, leaving at five-minute intervals.

passengers, two either side, in compartments which were well-upholstered and had wide picture windows. The LNER also brought out two-a-side first-class coaches in its improved coach sets for the 'Flying Scotsman'. Restaurant cars were furnished in Louis XIV style with free-moving armchairs, concealed lighting and hand-painted decor. In the adjoining kitchen cars Gresley, who pioneered electric cooking on trains in Britain, had installed electric refrigerators. All but the Southern introduced third-class sleeping cars in the late 1920s. Previously only first-class passengers had night berths; third-class passengers were given only a pillow and a rug.

Open-plan coaches were introduced not only because they carried more passengers but also because they were thought to appeal to third-class passengers by resembling the interior of road motor-coaches. At first only the LMS and LNER used them; the GWR regarded them, loftily, as only suitable for excursion trains and, other than as dining cars, barred them from scheduled services. The SR included part-open saloon accommodation in its express electric units.

The end of the 1930s saw the railways attaining new peaks in terms of public interest in the feats of express trains, even if not in terms of financial returns. In the face of increasing competition from road vehicles, air transport, diesel and electric traction, it seemed as though the steam locomotive was making a final determined bid to retain its supremacy. Part of that bid came in the form of the dramatic streamliners, with LNER leading the way. After high-speed trials in 1934 with improved Gresley A3 Pacifics, during which No 4472 reached the first undisputed 100mph in Britain and a sister engine 108mph a few months later, the LNER introduced a new train on a four-hour timing to Newcastle in the autumn of 1935. The train was named 'Silver Jubilee' in honour of King George V's 25 years on the throne and it was fully streamlined. In particular the silver-grey livery and the distinctive shape of Gresley's Pacific attracted attention. The wedge-shaped nose helped to carry smoke and steam clear of the cab windows apart from other aerodynamic considerations. However, underneath the streamlining the new A4 was not much different from the non-streamlined A3 Pacific, though slightly more powerful. In ordinary daily service the 'Silver Jubilee' could maintain only a maximum speed of 90mph, even though on a demonstration run in September 1935 it covered 70 miles at 90mph, 25 miles at 107mph and reached a peak of 112.5mph. However, in daily service it was still much faster than any other British train over comparable distances and an hour was cut from the previous journey time.

The 'Silver Jubilee's' success was followed with demands for a

L·N·E·R STREAMLINE TRAINS

MONDAYS TO FRIDAYS (will not run Friday 29th July to Monday 1st August inclusive)

"THE CORONATION"

Average throughout speed 65.5 m.p.h.
Accommodation limited to 210 passengers (48 First Class, 162 Third Class).

		p.m.			p.m.
King's Cross	...dep.	4. 0	Edinburgh (Waverley) ...dep.		4.30
York	... ,,	6.40	Newcastle ... ... ,,		6.33
Newcastle ...	... ,,	8. 0			
Edinburgh	...arr.	10. 0	King's Cross ...arr.		10.30

Connecting trains at Edinburgh, Newcastle and York.

"THE SILVER JUBILEE"

Average throughout speed 67.08 m.p.h.
Accommodation limited to 183 passengers (58 First Class, 125 Third Class).

		a.m.			p.m.
Newcastle ...	...dep.	10. 0	King's Cross ...dep.		5.30
Darlington ...	... ,,	10.42	Darlington ...arr.		8.48
		p.m.			
King's Cross	...arr.	2. 0	Newcastle ... ... ,,		9.30

Connecting trains serve Tyneside and Tees-side.

"WEST RIDING LIMITED"

Average throughout speed between Leeds and London 67.9 m.p.h.
Accommodation limited to 210 passengers (48 First Class, 162 Third Class).

		a.m.			p.m.
Bradford	...dep.	11.10	King's Cross ...dep.		7.10
Leeds	... ,,	11.31	Leeds ...arr.		9.53
		p.m.			
King's Cross	...arr.	2.15	Bradford ... ... ,,		10.15

Connecting trains at Leeds.

SUPPLEMENTARY FARES (for each single journey).

						1st Class s. d.	3rd Class s. d.
London and Bradford	...	...	...	...	...	4 0	2 6
London and Darlington	...	...	...	...	...	5 0	3 0
London and Edinburgh	...	...	...	...	...	6 0	4 0
London and Leeds	...	...	...	...	...	4 0	2 6
London and Newcastle	...	...	...	...	...	5 0	3 0
London to York	...	...	...	...	...	4 0	2 6
Newcastle and Edinburgh	...	...	...	...	...	3 0	2 0
York to Newcastle	...	...	...	...	...	3 0	2 0
York to Edinburgh	...	...	...	...	...	4 0	2 6

Seats can be reserved in advance through any of the Company's Passenger Agencies or Stations.

Built for the accelerated services to Scotland in the late 1930s, Stanier's 4–6–2 Duchess class Pacifics were very successful engines. The streamlined versions were painted in blue and silver or, as with No 6225 *Duchess of Gloucester* seen here passing through Rugby, in red and gold. (P B Whitehouse collection)

similar service to Edinburgh but the LMS would have preferred to concentrate generally on improving all services rather than introducing one crack express. Even so, when a high-speed service to Edinburgh was mooted, the LMS had to protect its Glasgow service. After trials with Princess Pacific No 6201, which had worked an eight-coach set from Glasgow to Edinburgh in $5\frac{3}{4}$ hours, the LMS introduced a high-speed train to Glasgow in the summer of 1937, using a larger streamlined Pacific. In view of the test performance by No 6201 *Princess Elizabeth*, the schedule of $6\frac{1}{2}$ hours set for this new 'Coronation Scot' train was considered unduly cautious, particularly when compared with the LNER's proposal to run its 'Coronation' express to Edinburgh in six hours.

The first LMS streamlined Pacific, No 6220, was also named *Coronation* and it had a slightly larger boiler than the LNER's A4. Though the gradients on the West Coast route were steeper than on the East, the locomotives were well matched in terms of speed and capability. Aerodynamically the rounded streamlining of the nose of the *Coronation* might have been better than the wedge of the A4 but it did not carry smoke and steam away from the cab as effectively. Engine and coach set were painted blue with silver lines extending from the front of the engine to the rear brake van. The LNER A4s for the 'Coronation' train were also blue with red wheels, while the

left:
A 1938 summer timetable giving details of the LNER's streamlined trains. (P B Whitehouse Collection)

coaches had Marlborough blue on the top half and Garter blue below.

The LMS *Coronation* left Euston on 29 June 1937 for a demonstration run of the 'Coronation Scot' to Crewe and back. Naturally the company did not want to be left out of the publicity which the LNER had gained when *Silver Link* had reached 112.5mph for the LNER, followed by 113mph by *Silver Fox* in 1936. Unfortunately, the LMS had no stretch of line as suitable as the LNER's Stoke Bank and had to be content with the descent to Crewe from Whitmore. That, however, left precious little distance in which to stop the train from a high speed.

After passing Stafford *Coronation* was opened out and passed Whitmore at 85mph. Speed built up rapidly and near milepost 156 it was estimated on stop watches to be 113mph – the same as *Silver Fox*. But the locomotive's speedometer recorded 114mph and, despite the possibility of inaccuracy, the record was claimed by the LMS. *Coronation* was still accelerating when steam was shut off and the train had just two miles to run into Crewe station. Flames were seen coming from the brake blocks as the train slowed rapidly, rattling alarmingly over points and sending crockery flying before halting safely at platform 3.

Although the record went to the LMS it had to be acknowledged that the LNER's 'Coronation' train was the more exciting in general performance. The 'Coronation Scot' could keep time with maximum speeds of no higher than 83–85mph; the 'Coronation' travelled at up to 90mph and occasionally went over 100mph to a top recorded speed of 107mph. The daily booking of 157 minutes, start-to-stop, from Kings Cross to York, 188.3 miles, was the fastest ever scheduled for steam in Britain.

A third streamliner was added by the LNER in the autumn of 1937 with the 'West Riding Limited' from Kings Cross to Leeds. The LMS did not introduce any similar trains for the London to Manchester or Liverpool service and instead made all-round improvements to the speed and frequency of ordinary services.

It was these two long-time rivals who figured in the peaks of achievement by British steam locomotives in the last two years of peace. While carrying out brake tests down Stoke Bank on 3 July 1938 the LNER A4 Pacific No 4468 *Mallard*, hauling 240 tons, reached a sustained speed of 125mph and peak of 126mph. Although the speeds were attained downhill, this was a world record for steam and *Mallard* was a smaller engine than others in the United States and Germany which had achieved over 120mph.

The LMS record was not one of speed but of power. In February 1939 the non-streamlined Pacific No 6234 *Duchess of Abercorn* ran on the Crewe–Glasgow main line with 20 coaches weighing 610 tons. A drawbar horsepower of over 2500 was recorded in the dynamometer car and the officially calculated indicated horsepower in the cylinders was over 3500. This, too, was a British record and both performances remain unsurpassed by steam.

The two locomotives, *Mallard* and *Duchess of Abercorn*, each had double chimneys, which improved their performances in two ways: by permitting better draughting, which raised more steam, and by reducing back pressure because exhaust steam escaped more freely. The double chimney was later used to good purpose in reducing coal consumption during and after the war which was effectively to put an end to the golden years of steam.

Gresley's one time *Hush Hush* high-pressure 4-6-4 as rebuilt and streamlined at Kings Cross in 1939.

right:
During the last five years of the 1930s there was considerable competition over the West Coast route to Scotland (LMS) and the East Coast route (LNER). Here is the LNER's 'Coronation' express crossing the Royal Border Bridge at Berwick. (E R Wethersett)

WORLD WAR II AND ITS AFTERMATH

The outbreak of World War II on 3 September 1939 was not un-expected and plans for centralised control of the railways in readiness for mass movement of troops, military equipment and civilian evacuation had been prepared during the previous 12 months. Two days before the formal declaration of war the Government took control of the four main-line railways as well as the London Passenger Transport Board and five minor railways. As in World War I, this action was taken through a Railway Executive Committee which on this occasion was made up by the general managers of the four main railways and of the LPTB. The executive had its headquarters in a disused tube station in the heart of London but those of the main-line railways were moved to various country mansions in the first weekend of September.

The first four days of the war saw the successful completion of one of the most remarkable mass passenger transport movements in all railway history: over 600,000 civilians (most of them children) were evacuated from London in 1577 special trains and more than 700,000 others from 17 other major centres of population in England and Scotland were moved out in a further 2246 trains.

Once again the passenger service was drastically curtailed and timings slowed down. In some cases journey times were even longer than at the height of World War I. Throughout the railway system speed limits were operated to conserve fuel and reduce maintenance needs. The famous named expresses and streamliners were taken off 'for the duration' and, as it transpired, the latter never returned. In 1940, after the deceptive calm of the 'phoney war', the railways were called upon to become involved in the military operation of the evacuation of Dunkirk. Between 27 May and 4 June nearly 300,000 British soldiers who had been rescued off the beaches of Dunkirk were transported from the Channel ports in 565 special trains, of which 327 ran from Dover. Having expected to have to cope with only about 30,000 men, the railway staff carried through a feat of improvisation which was extraordinary as well as unique. A further 200 special trains were laid on early in June to carry survivors from the western ports of France to reception areas which had been set up in the West Country.

The Dunkirk railway operation served as a dramatic warning of the sort of pressure under which the system was soon going to have to operate. Not only were the railways called upon to carry a mounting burden of freight traffic and to muster extremely long passenger and goods trains, they also became targets for the German bombers. Although the number of passenger trains had been reduced and civilians were again urged not to travel – 'Is your journey really necessary?' was a slogan of the time – thousands of military personnel were daily being transported about the country. The extra numbers generated huge trains and on the East Coast main line at least one 25-coach train was run from Kings Cross.

The pressure on freight services rose dramatically, not so much in terms of numbers of trains as in the need for more efficient loading, a loss of staff to the Forces and a decline in the standard of rolling stock because of the impossibility of keeping up with maintenance requirements. The traditional movement of much freight by night had to continue but now, because of the blackout, it was done with the

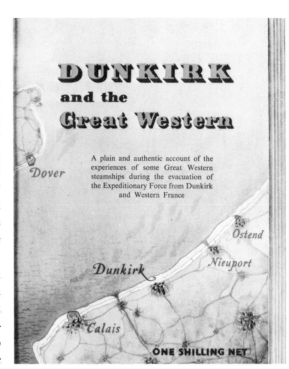

Home from Dunkirk – a village turns out to welcome one of the many trains transporting the evacuated troops from the coast. A GWR picture. (P B Whitehouse Collection)

were ready for occupation, transport the personnel. The LNER estimated that it had run 460 special trains to take the men to the East Anglian bases. Nor was that the end of the requirement, for when the air operations got under way the railways carried the munitions and fuel. A thousand-bomber raid required 28 fuel trains and eight bomb-carrying trains.

The greatest pressure of all came from the D-Day invasion and the build-up to it. From 26 March 1944 until the start of the invasion offensive on 6 June the railways had to run 24,459 special trains. In the week before D-Day there were 3636 extra trains to be scheduled,

Ex-LBSCR I2 class 4–4–2T as WD No 72401 stands forlornly at Guildford in January 1949 after use on the Longmoor Military Railway, Hants. (P M Alexander)

minimum of light. Despite all these difficulties net ton mileage had risen 43 per cent by 1943 compared with peacetime levels. This was achieved in spite of the intensive attacks on the railways by German bombers, principally in the 'Blitz' of 1940–41 but also with the V1 'doodle-bug' flying bombs and the V2 rockets. As soon as damage to railway property – particularly the permanent way and signalling – was reported, 'flying squads' of railwaymen were rushed to the scene to carry out immediate repairs, often working while air raids continued around them and bombs still fell.

As the tide of the war changed, the railways became involved in the RAF's preparation for the day-and-night air offensive against German targets. The massive construction programme for 150 new bomber airfields in East Anglia and new fighter bases in Kent and Sussex meant that the railways had, first, to carry the building materials to country stations near each site and then, once the bases

Unlettered with regard to ownership and with an undecipherable number, an 'Austerity' 2–8–0, built for the Government during the war, trundles a freight between Widney Manor and Knowle & Dorridge on 24 April 1948. (C F H Oldham)

left:
After World War II the SR acquired some former US Army Transportation Corps 0–6–0Ts as Southampton Docks shunters. (P M Alexander)

left:
A US Army Transportation Corps 2–8–0 No 1833 waits at Leicester Central towards the end of the war. (A W Flowers)

A diminutive LB & SCR A1X Class 0–6–0 Terrier tank still in Southern Railway livery leaves Havant with a Hayling Island train in March 1950. (P M Alexander)

right:
Because of restrictions on passenger travel due to the necessities of war the main line railways were not allowed to construct new express locomotives. The Southern – in dire need of new power – got over this by describing their 1941 built 'Merchant Navy' class pacifics as mixed traffic engines. Here is *Royal Mail Line* on its trial run on October 24th 1941. After the war this class became the Southern Region's heaviest express locomotive. (Millbrookhouse)

and in the four weeks after D-Day the demands became even more severe with the need to maintain essential supplies, carry forces' mail, lay on ambulance trains and carry incoming prisoners of war. The special train total in the four weeks after D-Day rose to over 18,000.

When the war ended in 1945 the railways were near breaking point and materially exhausted, with stock run down to the barest minimum and in desperate need of maintenance or replacement. The LMS calculated that £14 million was needed to catch up on arrears of maintenance on its tracks and signalling equipment and a further £26 million to bring the track back to acceptable peacetime standards. But that sort of money was not available to the railways, whose finances had been severely drained even before the war by the slump of the 1930s coupled with the drop in freight traffic because of competition from lorries. They had also invested heavily before the war in express passenger equipment. In 1938 only the GWR had been able to pay shareholders a dividend; the LNER's investors had received

West Highland shed: Fort William loco depot in 1953. Note that all engines are ex-LNER with a predominance of Gresley's K2 class 2–6–0s specially named for use on the West Highland line in the 1920/30s. Also on shed are ex-NBR Glen class 4–4–0s used in tandem with the 2–6–0s on most heavy trains. (P B Whitehouse)

When the Southern Railway electrified its main line (the old LSWR route) to Portsmouth it was not worth its while to deal likewise with the country branches *en route*. Here is Petersfield Junction in June 1951 with an LSWR M7 class 0–4–4 tank and push-and-pull train leaving from the little Midhurst branch platform which was on the opposite side of the level crossing from the main station. (P M Alexander)

right:
Watford Junction station with a semi-fast train from Euston to Bletchley. The engine is a LNWR Prince of Wales class 4–6–0 No 25752 in September 1946. (H C Casserley)

above:
Nottingham's Victoria station with a former GNR 4–4–0, LNER Class D2 No 2196, heading a branch train for Grantham in July 1947. (H C Casserley)

left:
Clouds tower over the east-bound 'Merchant Venturer' as it approaches Chippenham, Wiltshire. (G F Heiron)

right:
Still in her LMS wartime black livery underneath all the grime Stanier's formerly streamlined Duchess Class Pacific No 46247 *City of Liverpool* heads the London bound Mid-Day Scot away from Penrith in the early days of nationalisation. (Eric Treacy)

Stanier's ubiquitous 'Black Five' class 4–6–0 was probably one of Britain's most successful locomotives. They were seen hard at work from Bristol to Wick and gave particularly good service (often double-headed) on the main line to the old Highland Railway from Perth to Inverness. (W J V Anderson)

below:
The unusual sight of a King on a local train is explained by the fact that this Swindon–Bath–Swindon trip was a regular 'running in' turn for engines just out of Swindon works. Still with a single chimney, No 6002 *King William IV* climbs away from Box tunnel at Corsham, Wilts. (P M Alexander)

right:
The LMS at war – from a publicity poster made from a painting by Norman Wilkinson RA. (Crown Copyright National Railway Museum)

no return on their shares for four years. To add to their economic problems the Government failed to live up to its promise to reimburse the railways adequately for their work during the war. Indeed, the railways' revenue, which by 1942 was twice the annual payment of £43 million received from the Government, had been retained by Whitehall so that by 1945 the companies had actually lost money to the Government.

When a Labour Government was returned in 1945 it became inevitable that, despite a vigorous campaign by the four companies, the railways would be nationalised. Though several senior officers chose early retirement rather than work for an all-embracing Government-controlled system, the majority of railway employees greeted nationalisation with delight. The 1947 Transport Act covered all forms of transport and aimed at a co-ordinated system – an ideal that was not achieved. The British Transport Commission which took over on 1 January 1948 was established as corporate overlord of subordinate Transport Executives responsible for day-to-day management of main-line railways, public road transport, docks, canals, and London Transport.

As in the Grouping operation after World War I, the GWR again suffered little physical alteration; so did the Southern. They were changed to the Western and Southern Regions. However, the LMS

On the formation of British Railways it was deemed necessary to show unity as soon as possible by means of standard liveries for engines and coaches. In the event the most powerful passenger engines were painted blue (short-lived), lesser express engines GWR green, mixed traffic engines lined out black and others plain black. Here is *Coronation* class Pacific No 46248 *City of Leeds* in blue livery moving the fully loaded 15-coach 'Mid-day Scot' out of Euston station, bound for Glasgow. (G F Heiron)

A Great Central 4–4–2T, LNER Class C14 No 67442, on the old Cambrian/Great Western system at Oswestry in May 1949. This was the Wrexham–Oswestry auto service and the trailer car is GWR. The 4–4–2T was a Wrexham-based engine from the GCR/LNER-controlled Wrexham Mold & Connors Quay line of pre-nationalisation days. (P M Alexander)

Foreigner at work. A surprised car driver stares at LMS Duchess class Pacific No 46236 *City of Bradford* near Sidmouth Junction Southern Region during the Locomotive Exchange trials on 24 June 1948. (C F H Oldham)

and LNER were considered too long and widespread to be controlled as two Regions. Both surrendered their territory north of the border to the new Scottish Region; the LMS in the south became the London Midland Region and the LNER was divided into the Eastern and the North Eastern Regions. (In 1967 they were re-united into a single Eastern Region based at York.) The power vested in the pre-war railway management was not transferred to the new regional headquarters. Instead the Railway Executive exercised strict control from boardroom to 'track level' in every department.

Despite notable advances made in diesel traction in Germany and North America, the new Railway Executive made the momentous decision to continue with steam traction. Although after the war the LMS and LNER had decided to mount pilot main-line dieselisation schemes, only the LMS had actually started when the Railway Executive decided to develop a new range of standard, mainly mixed-traffic steam locomotives in seven power ranges up to express passenger Pacific status. One was a heavy freight class 9 2–10–0, the only earlier equivalent of which had been a wartime austerity design.

Waverley station, the Scottish terminus of the East Coast route, built by the North British Railway as it was in the early 1960s almost unchanged for over half a century. (Eric Treacy)

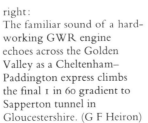

left:
In BR days A4 Pacific No 60028 *Walter K Whigham* hauls the 1950s 'Elizabethan' in a magnificent crescendo of sound as it emerges from Hadley Wood. (G F Heiron)

right:
The familiar sound of a hard-working GWR engine echoes across the Golden Valley as a Cheltenham–Paddington express climbs the final 1 in 60 gradient to Sapperton tunnel in Gloucestershire. (G F Heiron)

left:
Island Railway: The last remaining steam section on the Isle of Wight was the line from Ryde to Ventnor. Since early Southern days most passenger trains were worked by these Adams 0–4–4 tanks.

right:
Few London & North Western Railway passenger engines survived the Stanier era but World War II prolonged an odd lifespan. Here is one of the Prince of Wales class 4–6–0s to escape the torch until just after the war – No 25673 *Lusitania* at New Street station Birmingham. (P B Whitehouse)

above:
The Cambrian section of the former GWR was one of the first to be taken over by the new lightweight BR standard mixed traffic designs. Here is the up 'Cambrian Coast Express' climbing Talerddig bank behind the standard class 4 No 75005 in April 1956. (P B Whitehouse)

A South Wales named express – the 'Red Dragon' – races down the main line near Challow behind No 70029. (J F Russell Smith)

In fact the class 9 was used on fast passenger trains on occasions.

The LMS, in its preparation for the pilot scheme, had produced two prototype 1600hp main-line diesel-electric engines in 1947 and in the early 1950s the Southern Region was authorised to build three more, while the Western, ever striving for some measure of independence, experimented with two gas turbine-electric loco-motives, one of which was British and the other Swiss.

Britain was the only Western country to commit itself so heavily to steam in the post-war era. The decision lost British Railways the chance for orderly evaluation of various designs of diesel before steam was phased out and resulted in the costly and hectic rush into dieselisation with a variety of largely untried designs a few years later. The dogmatic attitude was one reason for the very slow progress made in Britain towards achieving the pre-war standards of train

During the early days of nationalisation and before steam became a dirty word, scientific tests were carried out with locomotives belonging to the old companies as well as BR's standard designs to measure and improve their performance. Here is an LNER V2 2–6–2 ('Green Arrow' class) under trials on the Western Region during the 1950s using the old GWR Dynamometer car. (P M Alexander)

LMS Jubilee class 4–6–0 No 45730 *Ocean* and BR Standard Class 6 Pacific No 72000 *Clan Buchanan* at Carlisle waiting for incoming trains from the south. (Eric Treacy)

left:
A few of the Standard 4–6–2s went to the Western Region. Here is No 70019 *Lightning* coupled in behind No 6010 *King Charles I* passing Aller Junction in July 1956. (C F H Oldham)

An early LMS 2–6–0, the Hughes 2–6–0 Crab No 42737 takes an empty goods train from Dalmellington to Ayr, Waterside, over the one-time Glasgow and South Western Railway. (Derek Cross)

below:
GWR King class 4–6–0 No 6002 *King William IV* at Wolverhampton, Stafford Road shed. (P B Whitehouse)

above:
Stanier's Duchess Pacific No 46240 *City of Coventry* at Shrewsbury loco depot after arriving on a running in turn from Crewe. (P B Whitehouse)

service. There was a serious shortage of good steam coal and, in addition, the attractiveness of a secure job on the railways which had been there before the war was diminished by the availability of many new, cleaner and better-paid employment opportunities. As a result steam depot staffs dropped below the official establishment level and there was a corresponding drop in maintenance.

In the final years of their independence the four major companies had embarked on steam construction programmes. The Southern had introduced new classes during the war with the attempt by its Chief Mechanical Engineer, O V S Bulleid to adapt the steam locomotive to the changing conditions. He came up with a new 4–6–2 design in which he combined a boiler of high steam-raising capacity with three cylinders and a chain-driven valve gear running in a closed oil bath. Rather than streamlining he employed 'air smoothing' by encasing the engine in metal sheeting – the intention as much as anything, being to save labour by cleaning the engines in carriage washing plants.

The first Bulleid 4–6–2 of 1941 was classed as a mixed-traffic type, to avoid a wartime ban on the construction of any passenger locomotives. The type proved capable of the highest speeds required and was produced in two classes, the large engines being named after

The driver watches from his cab for the green light as rebuilt Merchant Navy class No 35030 *Elder Dempster Lines* waits to head out of Waterloo with the 'Atlantic Coast Express' bound for Exeter and Ilfracombe. (G F Heiron)

Merchant Navy lines and the second, smaller and lighter engines bearing West Country and Battle of Britain names. In subsequent BR re-building the air-smoothing was removed. All LMR Pacifics were deprived of their streamlining. Only the Gresley A4s were allowed to survive as streamliners.

Railway operating methods in the first few years after nationalisation continued much as before and in many respects there might have

Southern Region's 'Merchant Navy' class 4–6–2 No 35029 *Ellerman Lines* leaving Templecombe with a West of England express. (P H Wells)

right:
A Jubilee takes a Cadbury's works excursion south in 1957. These mass visits to Cadbury's works at Bournville were a regular source of excursion traffic and were, at one time, very much encouraged by the railways. (Colourviews Picture Library)

The up Channel Islands Express passing Upwey Wishing Well (near Weymouth) behind Bulleid Pacific No 35003 *Royal Mail* June 1967. (Derek Cross)

As steam drew to an end on British Railways, surviving classes were dominated by the Standard engines; Britannia Pacific No 70028 *Royal Star* eked out her last days on freights and is seen here passing Kirkby Stephen on the Settle–Carlisle line. (Derek Cross)

600,000 privately owned wagons in use and most of these passed to British Railways. Whereas they had previously been used for the owners' purposes they now became available for multi-purpose use. However, there was a limiting factor in that many of the wagons were not fitted with power brakes controlled by the driver; most had mechanical handbrakes which were applied individually by shunters running alongside wagons and using poles to manipulate the brakes. The wagons with vacuum power brakes were mainly used to carry perishable goods on freight express trains. Trains without the advantage of controlled power braking throughout had to stop or slow to a crawl so that the handbrakes could be applied and pinned in the 'on' position, or else they relied only on the steam brake-power of the engine and the handbrake in the guard's van.

The role of the railway in a motor age received scant attention at first because the British Transport Commission had not unravelled the complexities of evolving a co-ordinated transport system before the General Election of 1952 put a Conservative Government in power. The Transport Act of 1953 not only denationalised much of the road transport industry but also began the abolition of BR's statutory charging and 'common carrier' obligations. This led the way to the market pricing and freedom to reject traffic which exist today. The Act also abolished the Executives and gave full responsibility for running the railways to the British Transport Commission. It was, however, a very rundown railway system, even though some services were getting back to pre-war standards.

seemed to have been few changes since the steam age was at its height. The variety of the loads carried by mixed freight trains continued to reflect the principle laid down in the Railway and Canal Traffic Act of 1854 of 'obligation to carry' all articles offered for transportation. Just as in pre-war days, most stations still had their goods shed and sidings which received at least a daily visit from a goods train. The transport of minerals – the reason that the Stockton and Darlington had been built in 1825 – remained an important revenue earner and in fact in the 125 years to 1950 the annual tonnage of coal carried by rail was well over half the total volume of freight. When the railways were nationalised in 1948 there were more than

4

MODERNISATION

DIESELISATION AND ELECTRIFICATION

Seven years after nationalisation the British Transport Commission was at last allowed by the Government to embark on a massive and very necessary re-investment programme. In 1955 it was given the go-ahead for a modernisation plan involving capital expenditure of £1240 million. Most of that money was to be used on new forms of tractive power and on modern rolling stock. At last, too, there was to be a national network of electrified lines spreading outwards from London. Electrification was scheduled for the East Coast route from Kings Cross to Doncaster, Leeds and York (possibly); for Euston to Birmingham, Liverpool and Manchester; for the Eastern Region line from Chelmsford to Ipswich taking in the Clacton, Harwich and Felixstowe branches. In addition the Kings Cross suburban system, the South Kent coast lines, the rest of Southern Region's main lines east of Reading and Portsmouth, and the Liverpool Street – north-east London suburban system were included in the electrification programme. Elsewhere steam locomotives were to be phased out and replaced by diesel locomotives and multiple-unit railcars. The BTC made the proviso that if it became possible to extend electrification still further, the dieselisation programme would be cut.

There was also, under the Modernisation Plan, to be major and much-needed expenditure on reconstructing the tracks which had been so well-worn during the war years and now had to be brought up to higher standards, on resignalling and on re-organisation of the freight business. More than one-quarter of the total investment capital was intended for the restructuring and modernisation of this important sector of the railway industry and most of the money was scheduled to go on new wagons, new or modernised marshalling yards and – at long last – on equipping all wagons with continuous brake systems. Regrettably, instead of opting for the efficient compressed air brake system, the Transport Commission took fright at the operating inconvenience of a changeover and decided to continue with the vacuum brake which, as stated earlier, had been fitted to a small proportion of goods vehicles before nationalisation. It was a decision which was to prove extraordinarily costly: in less than ten years a

change of policy made compressed-air braking standard for all new rolling stock so that thousands of new passenger and freight vehicles built with vacuum brakes in the meantime were obsolescent. Even more serious was the fact that new locomotives had been equipped with the now out-of-date system and were particularly costly to modify for air braking. Such was the cost of this serious error of judgment that even by the late 1970s, though all inter-city front-rank services were modernised with air braking, thousands of other vehicles were still either vacuum braked or had no continuous braking system.

The Plan was defective on other serious matters, particularly in the way it naively ignored the general economic state of the country which had considerable implications on the execution of the Plan and had a direct effect on the changing traffic patterns and rising costs. Its authors apparently could see no reason to reduce the size of the country's railway system or its operation and seemed to think that the panacea was to speed up services by using diesel or electric locomotives and installing electrically controlled colour-light signalling. Other 'cures' were to be the improved tracks, modern stations and new depots. At this stage, nobody thought to question whether all

A British Rail standard class 9F 2–10–0 No 92155 brings the empty stock of an excursion train into the platform at New Street station, Birmingham, in the summer of 1962.
(A W Flowers)

right:
The ubiquitous 9Fs. Probably the most successful of all the BR standard locomotive was the 9F 2–10–0. No 92135 moves slowly up to the starting signal at Westerleigh yards, Gloucestershire, before joining the main line with a north-bound freight.
(G F Heiron)

Castles at Shrewsbury in the early 1960s. On the left No 5072 *Hurricane* with a London to Birkenhead through train, whilst on the right an unknown Castle waits with another north-west bound express. (P B Whitehouse)

The Paddington–South Wales 'Red Dragon' headed by a BR standard class 7 4–6–2. (Colourviews Picture Library)

parts of the system were suitable for modernisation or even whether they were still needed.

Within three years the Plan was being re-appraised. Already the railways were running at an operating loss, costs were rising rapidly and freight traffic levels did not, because of upsets in industry, relate to forecasts. Problems were also growing on the re-equipment front. Before it was abolished, the Railway Executive had intended to carry out a thorough evaluation of 174 diesel locomotives in three broad power ranges. These were to have been grouped around selected depots and their individual records of performance, operating and maintenance costs studied closely so that each could be assessed as to potential for mass-production. The need for this somewhat tentative approach was because BR and the groups of pre-nationalisation days lacked diesel experience, though there were the five main-line

diesels evolved by the LMS and SR in the background.

These five apart, British diesel locomotive manufacture had been mainly in the form of limited, custom-built orders for overseas railways. The diesel types for this market were not considered to be readily adaptable to BR traffic requirements. Though the American railroads had wide experience of diesels and the United States could offer a well-tried diesel locomotive industry, political pressure in Britain prevented advantage being taken of this obvious solution to BRs problems. British diesel manufacturers were crying out for the opportunity to get in on the market so that they could gain experience of main-line diesel locomotive construction and turn it to advantage in breaking into the overseas market. Several diesel manufacturers, incidentally, were descended directly or through mergers and acquisitions, from pioneer steam locomotive builders:

English Electric, for example, included among its constituent companies Robert Stephenson & Company.

The Western Region, which since nationalisation had striven to retain a degree of independence, eventually persuaded the BTC to allow it to build German-patterned diesel-hydraulic locomotives under licence. Thus it was that the first Western Region main-line diesels presented a dramatic contrast to the diesels seen elsewhere on BR. The management of the Western had been impressed by the way in which German diesel manufacturers had achieved a successful combination of fast-running engines with hydraulic transmisssions and comparatively low all-up weight, to achieve a 2000 horsepower locomotive weighing just under 80 tons. This compared with the 130-or-more tons of the diesel-electric locomotives which BR was considering. The German design was modified to meet the more restricted BR loading gauge and production began, with engines and transmission initially being imported from Germany.

Here it should be explained that there are basically three types of transmission for the power produced by a diesel engine: mechanical, through a fluid coupling, gearbox and final drive; electrical, with the engine driving an electric generator to provide current for electric traction motors; and hydraulic, through one or more torque convertors, with a fluid coupling between the drive and the driven mechanism. Electric transmission had the longest record of service and had been adopted by American railroads in the 1930s. They were the most attractive proposition to BR Regions which had electric lines because there already existed workshops to maintain electric traction equipment.

The trials of the 174 various diesel locomotives were never completed because, faced with a rapidly deteriorating financial situation, the BTC decided it must scrap steam and go straight into a programme of rapid dieselisation. The Commission was also faced, in reaching its decision, with a growing shortage and rising price of good steam coal and with the difficulty of recruiting good footplate and maintenance staff prepared to work in the dirty conditions which inevitably surrounded steam locomotion.

In the rush to dieselisation the BTC placed orders in 1957 for the mass production of several diesel types – in some cases prototypes had not even been completed. Such was the speed at which the BTC wanted to carry through its programme of dieselisation that in five years from the end of 1958 to 1963 the BR stable of motive power completely altered in make-up. At the beginning of that period BR had 16,108 steam locomotives, 105 main-line diesels and 2417

left:
Oliver Bulleid's Southern
Region 0–6–6–0 Leader class
experimental locomotive
performs on trial. This class
never entered regular
service. (Cecil J Allen
collection)

left:
The LMSR 'Ro-Railer' was
an experimental vehicle
which on reaching the rail-
head changed from its
flanged wheels to tyred
wheels and proceeded to its
destination by road. It is
seen here under test on the
Harpenden–Hemel
Hempstead branch in the
early 1930s. (C J Allen
collection)

Pre-war diesel experiment –
an articulated three-car
multiple-unit train built by
the LMS in 1938 and tried on
the Oxford–Bletchley–
Cambridge route. (R G
Jarvis)

multiple-unit railcars. In 1963 the picture had altered so that there were only 7050 steam locomotives left while the number of main-line diesels had risen to 2051, diesel railcars numbered 4145 and shunters, 2009.

Attempting to catch up with most of the rest of the world, BR inevitably encountered many shocks and problems because it was making a changeover which was without precedent in its scale. There were many difficulties from a variety of causes, including an initial lack of purpose-built maintenance depots and fully trained staff, a failure to appreciate the need for mass production of components to be carried out in scrupulously clean conditions and to high tolerances, and the realisation that the 2000–2500hp diesel-electric locomotives with 14- or 15-coach loads were not, after all, going to bring any dramatic reductions in the journey times which steam traction had established.

British Railways standard Britannia class 4–6–2 No 70025 Western Star with a mixed freight near Badminton in 1961. (Colourviews Picture Library)

below:
The Great Western Railway introduced these streamlined railcars during the 1930s to act as branch-line units and also (for example on the Birmingham to Cardiff run) to form a fast and compact inter-city service. (P B Whitehouse)

The 1955 Plan had proposed the electrification of 200 miles of the East and West Coast main lines from London to the north by 1970. It was quickly realised that this was a target beyond the capabilities of the industry and of BR's electrical engineering resources. Main-line electrification from Kings Cross was therefore shelved. Electrification was not new and the first English electric railway had been opened by Magnus Volk in Brighton in 1883. The North Eastern and the Lancashire & Yorkshire Railways were the first main-line companies to use this form of power in 1904 in Newcastle and Liverpool. The pioneer deep-level tube railway in London had opened in the 1890s and was followed by extensions and new lines at the beginning of the twentieth century. The early electric schemes used direct current at 600–650 volts, the supply being fed through conductor rails outside the running rails. Some systems had a single conductor rail which carried the positive current with the return supply through the running rails at earth potential; others had a fourth insulated rail in the middle of the track to carry the return supply. The pioneer London Underground lines had electric locomotives but the main-line companies worked their electric suburban services with motor coaches which were capable of being controlled as a complete unit from the leading cab. Thus was born the multiple-unit system.

It was the Midland Railway which, in 1908 and 1909, introduced alternating current on its lines between Lancaster, Morecambe and Heysham. The 6600-volt current was collected from an overhead wire and the supply transformed to a lower voltage in the motor

right:
A Western Region diesel hydraulic locomotive No D1013 *Western Ranger* at Paddington station on the arrival of an express from the West of England. (Eric Treacy)

The north wind blows across the exhaust of No 18000 one of the Western Region's two gas turbine locomotives at Bristol Temple Meads in January 1952. (P M Alexander)

left:
A Plymouth–Edinburgh express passes over the Royal Border bridge at Berwick-on-Tweed behind a class 40 English Electric locomotive No D625 in 1972. (D Cross)

Newcastle Central station, Eastern Region in March 1970. This train carrying cars bound for the north is hauled by a diesel-electric locomotive of class 40, No D274. (Derek Cross)

Early overhead suburban electrification – London & Brighton, South Coast train in Victoria Station. (C J Allen collection)

In 1909 the London, Brighton & South Coast Railway opened its AC electrification system on its line between London Bridge and Victoria, thereby responding to the competition of the tramways. This line used 6700 volts AC at 25 Hz from an overhead line. The system was extended to Coulsdon on the Brighton line, and Sutton on the Dorking and Horsham line, by 1928. Meanwhile the LNWR inaugurated conductor electrification at 630 volts DC in 1914 on its Willesden–Earls Court branch. This was the first stage of the company's conversion of suburban lines between Broad Street, Euston and Watford. The London & South Western followed a year later with 660-volt DC, third-rail electrification on suburban lines from Waterloo, an event which was later to be of importance for railways in Southern England. Also in 1915 the North Eastern introduced electric working on the Shildon–Newport line in County Durham. The NER adopted 1500 volts DC with overhead collection and trains were hauled by locomotives of the double-bogie type with traction motors mounted on the axles. (Today they would be described as having a Bo-Bo wheel arrangement on the basis that 'A' stands for one driving axle of a group, 'B' means two, etc, and that the suffix 'o' denotes independent motors on each axle.)

With the variety of electrification systems in use after World War I, standardisation was desirable and direct current seemed to be favoured. After Grouping, Herbert Walker, who had been General Manager of the LSWR and took up the same post for the Southern, brought in a 660-volt DC third-rail system as standard for the SR. By 1930 the company had virtually completed its electrification schemes in the London suburban area and with nearly 900 track-miles was able to claim 'the world's greatest suburban electrification'. Then came plans to extend electrification to the South Coast, starting with Brighton and Worthing. This was regarded as an extended suburban electrification scheme rather than a main-line one, and the 660-volt DC system was therefore retained. The work was completed by the end of December 1932. All services ran with multiple-unit stock, the Brighton non-stop trains being formed from six-car units, each with a Pullman car. The Southern boasted the only electric multiple-unit Pullman trains in the world and the Pullman Car Company built three five-car all-Pullman sets for the famous 'Brighton Belle' service. The 'Belle' continued until 30 April 1972.

The Southern continued to extend its electrification by turning to the former LBSCR lines between 1933 and 1938 and at the same time converting other sections. In the east of its territory the supply reached Sevenoaks in 1935 and the Medway towns in 1939; the

The LNWR four-rail London surburban electrification of 1914 was extended to Watford and also over the District line. Two of the three-car sets wait at Richmond Station in 1925. (H G W Household)

coaches before being fed to the traction motors. On the Continent and in the United States high-voltage alternating current was being developed at the same time but successful traction by alternating current motors could only be achieved with frequencies below the standard 50 cycles per second (now referred to as 50 Hertz or 50 Hz), so the Midland generated its own supply at 25 Hz. The debate on the relative advantages of AC or DC supply for electric traction has continued ever since.

route from Waterloo to Portsmouth Harbour was completely electrified by July 1937; and on New Year's Day 1939 the Waterloo–Reading and Guildford via Ascot services began electric working. The Southern's concentration on electrification made its service popular with the commuting public in its territory. Though the topography of the area made dramatic improvements in journey times impossible, the company provided regular services at standardised departure times. The London–Brighton non-stop trains, for example, were then advertised as 'on the hour in the hour' (the 55-minute schedule came later). Such a service proved a better selling point than crack named trains and set the pattern for today's high-speed Inter-City services.

Elsewhere the first new electrification scheme to be completed after the Pringle Report – the report of one of several committees set up to recommend standards of electrification – was that for the Manchester South Junction and Altrincham joint line of 1927 which used 1500 volts DC with overhead contact wires. It was the first passenger-carrying line to use this voltage which was later accepted as standard for main-line electrification in Britain (except on the Southern) until BR changed to 25,000 AC at 50 Hz in 1956. Although the NER had planned in 1919 to electrify the York–Newcastle line on the 1500-volt DC overhead system and actually built a 4–6–4 (2–C–2 in today's classification) electric locomotive, the project was abandoned with the approach of Grouping. In the following decade the LNER drew up plans for the electrification of the Manchester–Sheffield–Wath line through the Woodhead Tunnel across the Pennines and actually started work. Another scheme envisaged electrification of the suburban lines between Liverpool Street and Shenfield. Both schemes were on the 1500-volt DC system. Progress was interrupted by World War II but the Shenfield scheme was eventually completed by BR in 1949 and the Manchester–Sheffield–Wath in 1954.

It was against this background that in 1951 the BTC reaffirmed its faith in the 1500-volt DC overhead wire system and authorised extensions to the Liverpool Street–Shenfield scheme to Chelmsford and Southend. Even so, the Commission had been impressed by the findings of yet another committee set up to survey world development of electric traction and it ordered a trial conversion of the Lancaster–Morecambe–Heysham line to high-voltage AC electrification using the 50 Hz industrial supply frequency. The front-runners in this technique were the French, who by the mid-1950s had found it so successful in terms of economical running, of installa-

The third-rail electrified system out of London's southern termini was developed during the inter-war years into one of the world's most intensively used suburban systems. Here is an early Southern multiple-unit formation near Bromley in 1938. (H C Casserley)

Electric Pullman: One of Britain's best-known trains was the old 'Southern Belle' renamed 'Brighton Belle' – an all-electric Pullman express with luxury now superceded by expediency. Here the 'Belle' enters Brighton in 1948. (P M Alexander)

Dieselisation made its first impact when DMU sets began to replace steam suburban trains on the BR system. Here in 1961 the 1.15 pm (13.15) Wellington (Salop) to Lapworth train waits to leave Birmingham's Snow Hill station. This station is now closed, the tracks torn up and buildings demolished. (M Mensing)

The down Bournemouth Belle departs from Southampton 50 minutes late double headed by type 3 diesel electric locomotive No D6549 and Battle of Britain class 4–6–2 No 34077 after the steam locomotive had become incapable of hauling the train beyond Farnborough. The locomotive was retained to provide steam heating. The date was 29 December 1966 – some six months before the final demise of steam on that route.

left:
Egton station, Yorkshire, in March 1970. The train is ex-Middlesborough–Whitby diesel multiple unit. (Derek Cross)

tion costs and of providing excellent traction, that the BTC this time took note of overseas experience and adopted the 25,000-volt (25kV) 50 Hz supply for all future electrification. The only exception, as we have mentioned, was the Southern Region, which retained the third-rail system, though increasing the supply from 660 volts to 750 volts DC when equipment renewals were due. This system was so widely used in the region that it would not have made economic sense to attempt conversion.

On the London Midland, AC electrification continued with the completion of the Manchester–Crewe section in September 1960. The system was gradually extended in the region, first from Liverpool to Crewe and then south to Nuneaton. It eventually reached Euston in 1966. A year later lines in the Birmingham area and from Rugby to Stafford were added and by 1974 the whole of the West Coast route north of Crewe to Glasgow, over Shap at Beattock had been converted. Suburban schemes such as those around Glasgow and in the north and east of London from Liverpool Street (including the main line to Clacton) and Fenchurch Street to Southend, were also changed over. Some inner suburban lines were at first supplied with 6250 volts, the trains being converted to work on this lower voltage as well as the full 25,000 volts. Automatic equipment was installed so that the voltage changeover was initiated at the boundary between the two supplies. It was thought at first that the 25 kV system required

at least an 11-inch clearance above and below the contact wire to avoid flashovers and this would have required the rebuilding of hundreds of bridges. The lower voltage obviated much of this reconstruction work. In fact it was later found that 11-inches was over-cautious and clearances were reduced. At the same time the go-ahead was given to abandon the lower voltage in future. To give full compatability, the lines from Liverpool Street which were originally electrified at 1500 volts DC were converted to AC in readiness for electrification extensions on high voltage alternating current. All these electrification schemes and some non-electric trunk routes were completely resignalled with colour-light signals and, in most cases, control from centralised power signalboxes which are in charge of long lengths of line.

British Rail's alternating current electrification schemes were not without problems. Soon after the commissioning of the Manchester–Crewe section in 1960 massive rises in construction costs so frightened Parliament that the project was stopped while the finances were examined. The problems lay not only in inflation but also in all the extras, like station rebuilding, which were not essentials of electrification but had been thrown in as part of the overall scheme. Additionally, there had been little real appreciation of the savings which electrification could bring by way of track simplification; much of the conversion was carried out on the basis of what was already there, rather than on what was really needed. There were also major equipment faults which brought the Glasgow scheme and those in north and east London to a halt and took many months to sort out.

In the diesel field, too, it was not until the mid-1960s that the results of the rush to dieselisation were unravelled and some order and a greater measure of reliability were obtained. Prototype diesel locomotives which had been brought in without proper trials were replaced and new construction was standardised on single diesel-electric designs in each of four power ranges. Meantime the Western Region had succeeded in maintaining its independent air and had expanded its diesel-hydraulic main-line fleet to four types. Of these the most imposing and largest was the 2700hp class 52 Western. The region all the time faced strong opposition from BR's chiefs and from industry because of the German involvement. Finally, in the face of claims against their high initial and maintenance costs and allegedly chronic failure records, the diesel-hydraulics were condemned by the railway hierarchy in favour of locomotives with diesel-electric transmission. These were, it was insisted, more robust and capable of sustaining medium high speed at lesser cost. BR headquarters ordered the end of diesel-hydraulic construction and the conversion of the Western to diesel-electric. Total elimination of the hydraulic version took 15 years.

The new standard high-powered diesel-electric was the class 47 with six powered axles. Introduced as a 2750hp, 95mph locomotive weighing 114 tons, the unit was found to be subject to stresses and had to be derated to 2580hp. Only 22 British Railways locomotives existed until the mid-1960s which were capable of fulfilling the inter-city speed estimates contained in the 1955 Plan. They were the 3300hp class 55 Deltics made by English Electric which were so named because the company had designed them round the delta-shaped 18-cylinder, opposed-piston Napier engine which had originally been developed for high-speed naval craft. English Electric had constructed a prototype speculatively and demonstrated its capabilities of speed and power – which were almost of electric-style proportions – on BR main lines in 1959. The BTC then agreed that the East Coast route should have a fleet of the Deltics to compensate for its frustrated hope of electrification. However, there were possible weaknesses about the proposals to introduce the Deltic in terms of its high initial cost and its complexity; there were also objections to the fact that the BTC was resorting to an engine which had previously been untried on rail. Because of these objections the Deltic was brought into service under a contract which provided that English

Drem Junction in June 1972 with an afternoon London to Edinburgh express behind Deltic D9017 *The Durham Light Infantry*. (Derek Cross)

Electric maintained the engines, largely on the basis of a pool of replacement spare assemblies. The Deltics on the East Coast route, and the LMR electric locomotives were the leaders of British Rail's express services which were introduced in the late 1960s under the name 'Inter-City' with well-publicised daily 100mph speeds over suitable sections of track.

Even in the first half of the 1960s there was alarm at the mounting BR losses. The politicians stepped in and a committee – the Stedeford Committee, after its Chairman, Sir Ivan Stedeford – was set up to examine the future role of railways and how they were to be financed and administered. A member of that committee was Dr Richard Beeching, who was then technical director of Imperial Chemical Industries (ICI). The Transport Act 1963 paved the way for the British Railways Board which had been recommended by the Stedeford Committee. Dr Beeching was appointed first Chairman of the Board and was to write his name into railway history.

English Electric Type No 3 37–050 trundles under Hawkshead Bridge at Brookmans Park with a train of empty hoppers heading South. (P. J. Howard)

A West Coast main line express races northwards behind a class 86 electric locomotive. (Eric Treacy)

THE HIGH SPEED AGE BEGINS

The new British Railways Board and its chairman, Dr Beeching, took a searching look at the railways system under its control and soon appreciated that widespread changes were needed. Beeching found that about half the system carried roughly 95 per cent of traffic, while the other half carried the remainder. With local bus routes then able to serve most rural areas more efficiently than railways and with the great increase in private car ownership since the end of the war, many lines which were lossmakers clearly had to be closed and small intermediate stations on main lines were shut.

Closures of unremunerative services were not new. Some went in World War I, others in the 1930s, and BR had gradually accelerated closures in the 1950s. But none of this had the widespread effects of the sweep of the axe which was to follow the Beeching examination. As chief author of the *Reshaping Report* issued by the British Railways Board, Beeching lopped branches, cross-country lines and even one or two main lines. Among major casualties were the Midland & Great Northern and Somerset & Dorset joint lines and the Great Central London extension main line, opened as recently as 1899. Gone too were the North British main line from Carlisle to Edinburgh, the Midland main line from Derby to Manchester and the original Midland Counties line from Rugby to Leicester which was part of the first route from Euston to the North East.

On the traffic side, local stopping passenger trains ceased on many routes as there were no local stations left for them to serve. The greatest changes were made on the freight side. Beeching was convinced that the principal role of the railway was as a bulk carrier and that freight should be organised on a trainload rather than a wagonload basis.

The handling of small consignments of packages and crates was one of the biggest lossmakers and since road transport was involved at some stage of almost every freight operation it was thought that small consignments would be best left to the road transport industry, collecting and delivering from centrally placed sundries depots, with trunk rail haulage in trainloads between depots far apart. Other freight was to be carried in containers, with road collection and

Brought in at the end of the 1950s to rationalise the railway system. Dr Richard (now Lord) Beeching, once of ICI, set about his task with considerable thoroughness. The present track mileage is almost unchanged from the final wielding of his axe. (John Adams)

left:
Edinburgh Waverley station with class 55 Deltic No 9018 *Ballymoss* at the head of the up 'Flying Scotsman'. (Eric Treacy)

delivery at the start and finish of the journey and high-speed, long-distance rail haulage in between in special 75mph Freightliner container trains. Coal for power stations was carried by block trains of hopper wagons designed to be loaded at pitheads and unloaded automatically at the destination as they continued to move slowly. In this way two or three trains could be handled in a working day, providing a service which was virtually non-stop. Indeed, they soon acquired the name-tag 'merry-go-round trains' and presented a great contrast to the days just passed when wagons spent much time being sorted in marshalling yards and waiting to be loaded or unloaded. Domestic coal movement was re-organised to run as block loads to centralised coal distribution depots; other bulk traffic carried in block trains included oil, chemicals, fertilizer, aggregates and car components.

The effect of running so much traffic as through trains from one originating point to a single destination was to reduce dramatically the number of trains needing to be remarshalled, and in turn reduce the use of many marshalling yards, some of which had been built or enlarged only a few years before. Many became 'white elephants', as did such structures as the flyover at Bletchley, which had been built in the 1960s to carry freight trains over the electrified West Coast main line on to a planned new ring route avoiding London – a route which, in the event was no longer necessary.

Another more positive feature of the new regime was the introduction of new high-capacity wagons, among them long-wheelbase four-wheel vans of up to 45 tons capacity (fully loaded) and massive bogie tank wagons with a loaded weight of 100 tons. All were fully equipped with power brakes and capable of running at speeds of 60–75mph.

Since the mid-1960s successive governments had been far more involved in the way British Railways had been run because of the financial losses which were being incurred despite closures of uneconomic lines and more progressive modernisation of the remainder. Closures were not always the answer, for lossmaking services carried valuable traffic as feeders to otherwise profitable main lines, while many suburban services around cities – Southern electric services around London, for example – fulfilled essential social needs. The principle of grant payments by Government or local authorities was accepted to support essential passenger services which were loss-making. Moreover, the Government through the Department of Transport and the Treasury, has had to approve and sometimes give financial assistance for new works such as the new electrification

Class 55 Deltic No 55.–009 as D9009 *Alycidon* with the down 'Flying Scotsman' passes York. (Eric Treacy)

tive, as, for example, the faster more frequent passenger services and the better outlook for bulk freight by rail. Overall policy control by the politicians had come to stay though, whichever Government was in power and whatever its political views on transport. Indeed, the 1970s, despite frustration arising from the economic state of the country as a whole, were to prove as exciting for rail transport in Britain as the first railways had been 150 years before. A growing energy crisis, in which oil shortages were becoming serious and were accompanied by ever-increasing prices, was beginning to show the economic advantages of rail over road transport. Further large-scale electrification schemes looked financially more attractive in such a context.

By the end of the 1960s, too, it was clear that the West Coast electric and East Coast Deltic diesel services, with their regular-interval frequency, top 100mph pace and 75–80mph averages (compared with 60mph by steam in the late 1950s) were succeeding in the battle for passengers against private cars on the new motorway network and airlines. Indeed, the commercial success of LMR electric and East Coast Deltic services soon brought calls from other routes for equipment capable of 100mph-plus maximum speeds and end-to-end averages of 80mph or more.

Improvements to track and signalling technology made possible at relatively small cost some improvements in services by eliminating features which had necessitated speed restrictions on some stretches. The East Coast main line was brought up to the standard required for continuous 100mph running, practically from London to Doncaster and for 85 miles of the remaining 112 to Newcastle. This was achieved by the Eastern Region in the early 1970s for an outlay of about £60 million and in 1976 it was possible for the 'Flying Scotsman' to improve its Kings Cross-Edinburgh timing to 5 hours 27 minutes, an average of 72.1mph and a best recorded route schedule of 80.8mph.

In the spring of 1974 the completion of the electrification of the West Coast main line from north of Crewe to Glasgow meant that the great climbs to the fells of the North of England and Scotland were reduced to comparatively minor pulls by the power of the locomotives. Shap and Beattock banks, with inclines of 1-in-74.5, which had tested the steam locomotives, now had the 'Royal Scot' roaring over them as it ran from London to Glasgow at an average speed of 80.3mph in a five-hour journey (including an intermediate stop at Preston). One result was that by the autumn of 1974 the route had carried over 50 per cent more passengers than in 1973.

schemes, resignalling programmes, large purchases of new loco-motives and rolling stock, and research.

It was against all the upheavals of the Beeching era, with a slimmer system getting to grips with new operating methods, that British Rail faced the 1970s. Steam traction had finally come to an end in regular service in 1968 and diesel and electric traction were emerging from their rather troubled starts. Not all of the Beeching period had been negative and demoralising. Some proposals were highly posi-

Modern track maintenance –
a Plasseur Mainline Universal
06.16 CTM tamper in
action on the up slow line
near Pirbright moving
"wrong line" to the West.
(Peter Howard)

coaches (third-class had been renamed second throughout most of Western Europe in 1956) were entirely of the open saloon type and the side-corridor compartment style was on its way out. Succeeding batches of Mark II coaches had improvements in detail including a change from vacuum to compressed-air braking. The fourth version, MkIID of 1972, was equipped with full air-conditioning and dispensed with opening windows in passenger saloons.

Air-conditioning had been used in five sets of diesel-electric Pullman multiple-units in the early 1960s built primarily to attract the

left:
New Street station, Birmingham during the chaotic period of rebuilding in the 1960s. (Colourviews Picture Library)

below:
A container is being transferred at a Freightliner terminal. Lorries collect and deliver the containers locally, leaving the trunk haul to rail. (British Railways)

Improvements in timings continued on all regions and in 1978 the LMR electric main line carried 165 trains daily with start-to-stop averages of 80mph or more, with a top of 88.8mph between Rugby and Watford Junction. In 1939 the whole British Railway network had 116 daily runs timed at an average of 60mph under steam.

British Rail discovered, as the SR had before, that regular-interval, or repeat-pattern train services were justified and economically viable. The public was offered more trains each day because the regular timetable structure made programming of men and equipment simpler and involved rapid turnrounds of locomotives, trainsets and crews at the terminals. Success of the system spurred BR into planning even faster trains and all-round improvements in passenger comfort. The original standard BR passenger coaches of the 1950s had introduced such features as all-steel construction and greater safety but the layout, seat design and decor had not advanced greatly for 25 years. Moreover, at speeds of more than 70mph the standard BR coach was noisy and hardly the best ride. In the mid-1960s a BR Mark II version appeared with new-style bogies which owed something to Continental practice. It rode fairly steadily up to 100mph and had a brighter interior, new seat designs and modern decor. Second-class

first-class business market. Known as the 'Blue Pullmans' for their blue-and-white livery in place of the traditional brown-and-cream, they were fixed-formation trains with a diesel-electric streamlined power car at each end which included passenger accommodation. There were kitchen and parlour cars between. Three eight-car sets for the Western Region included a small amount of second-class accommodation but the two six-car units used for the St Pancras–Manchester Midland Pullman were entirely first-class. Like all Pullmans on BR after 1954 they were entirely owned by the railway. A supplementary fare was charged on top of the ordinary fare. The cars were effectively sound-proofed and with modern decor and ergonomically designed seats they were far above the standards of ordinary BR trains and equal to the best in Europe. The 'Blue Pullmans' were intended to provide a luxury service at fairly high speeds – they were designed for 90mph top speeds – on routes paralleling the LMR West Coast route during disruption caused by electrification work. From 1967 all five sets were allocated to the Western Region for service between London and South Wales or the Midlands. Pullman services were on the way out for with improvements to ordinary standards they no longer offered so great an incentive in terms of improved comfort. The Southern Region finally abandoned Pullmans in 1972 and its South Coast services were given the role of being little more than outer-suburban in character. The 'Blue Pullmans' were withdrawn in 1973.

They had established the principle of a fixed-formation train with self-contained power cars needing no terminal locomotive movements and hence capable of quick turnrounds in the platform with servicing and kitchen restocking taking place at the same time. Similar advantages of quick turnrounds were achieved on the Glasgow–Edinburgh service in the early 1970s with fixed formation sets of coaches by two diesel locomotives, one at each end, and with multiple-unit control of both from the leading cab. They thus had all the flexibility of the lighter lower-powered diesel multiple-unit trains used on local services.

While all this was going on BR started research in the 1960s into new-generation trains going beyond the then known rail technology. Apart from a scientific approach to problems of wheel behaviour on rail at high speeds, research began into the concept of an Advanced Passenger Train, or APT, which, it was claimed would ride satisfactorily at up to 155mph on the straight and would be able to take curves 40 per cent faster than conventional trains without the need for modifications to existing main-line routes.

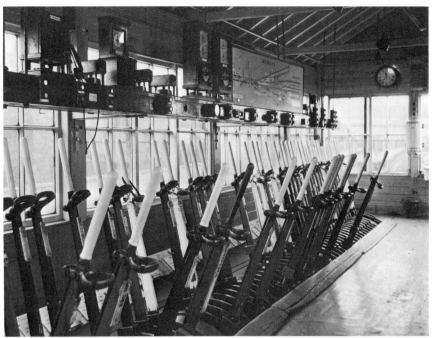

Until very recent times most signal boxes on the British Railway system were worked by signalmen using interlocked mechanical or electropneumatic lever frames with electric block instruments. Here is a signal box on the LMS Railway at Carlisle showing levers, block instruments and a track circuit diagram. (Colourviews Picture Library)

Wilmslow power box on the Manchester line of the London Midland Region. (British Railways)

Aerospace research played an important part in the design theory of the APT, in which it was proposed that a lightweight coach built using aerospace techniques, should embody a patent suspension system that enabled the wheels to steer round curved track as the coach body tilted automatically to the correct angle. The body-tilting system counteracted excessive effects of centrifugal force at high speed which might have upset passengers. In 1967, when the

West Coast electrification – a 25Kv AC electric train proceeds over brand new concrete sleepered track in 1976. (Eric Treacy)

right:
The *Talisman*, now a 125 HST, leaves Kings Cross with a class 31 No 31-201 in the background. (P J Howard)

left:
Watford Junction power signal box showing illuminated track diagram and control panel. (BR LM Region)

above right:
Permanent relaying with concrete sleepers at Hest Bank on the LM Region meets the increased and faster traffic on electrification. (Colourviews Picture Library)

project was unveiled, the British Railways Board optimistically announced that, if sufficient resources were made available to complete research and development, the first APTs could be running in service by 1972. Government money was made available in 1968 to meet half the estimated research and development cost but by 1972, when the first prototype APT took to the rails there had been some radical changes in design. In the meantime the railways were again, like the whole country, having financial problems and the Government was reluctant to put more money into a technology which was so far unproven.

Traditionalists in BR mechanical engineering felt that conventional trains still had greater potential and with commercial calls for more positive improvements the BRB agreed in 1970 to order a fresh development of the orthodox design in the form of the 125mph High-Speed Diesel Train or HST. When it emerged in 1972 the prototype proved to be a double-ended set of seven new Mk III coaches (at 75ft, longer than previous types) with a pair of 2500hp diesel-electric power cars. At almost the same time the prototype APT was unveiled: a four-car gas turbine-electric powered set.

Both prototype trains went on to set new British speed records during their trials. The HST reached 143mph on almost level track between Darlington and York on 11 June 1973; the APT touched 152mph between Reading and Swindon in August 1975.

Approval for mass production was given first to the HST and the initial batch went into service on the Western Region's Paddington–Bristol/South Wales routes in October 1976, after track and signalling improvements had been made to nearly 100 miles of route.

right:
Electric locomotives at Crewe station. The new 25,000-volt AC overhead system on the up-to-date West Coast main line has now been extended from London (Euston) to Birmingham, Manchester, Liverpool and Glasgow. (Eric Treacy)

View of New Street station, Birmingham, taken in 1962 showing a southbound express waiting to depart from platform 3. This view gives a clear indication of the umbrella roofing which spanned the construction period between the overall glass roof and the new station now in use. (Colourviews Picture Library)

Introduction of the service involved the setting of new 125mph standards for equipment and precise timetabling. The resulting passenger service was surpassed only by the famous Japanese New Tokaido Line for end-to-end speed and frequency. Significantly, the Japanese results are achieved on brand-new lines designed for and used by electric passenger trains whereas the Western Region's BR Inter-City 125 operation involved fitting in 48 125mph diesel trains each weekday with the existing traffic of an established railway service. City-to-city start-to-stop average speeds were of over 93mph between London and Newport and the exceptional acceleration of the HSTs allowed short sprints to be timed at a peak average of 103.3mph. The new service brought Bristol closer to London in travelling time than many outer suburban stations in the Southern Region and one result was that passenger carryings on the Western HST routes rose by one-third in the first two years of the Inter-City 125.

The second series of HSTs, including eight intermediate coaches, opened up a new service on the East Coast route in 1978. The 'Flying Scotsman's' time for the London–Edinburgh journey was cut to 4 hours 52 minutes, with an average of 87.7mph to the first stop at Newcastle. That timing was further improved after the full allocation

A multi-aspect colour-light signal. (Colourviews Picture Library)

The mid-1960s found the main West Coast route from London to Birmingham, Manchester, Liverpool and Glasgow electrified by the 25,000-volt AC overhead system giving a frequency of service hitherto unrealized. A Manchester express about to depart from London (Euston) behind AL6 class (now class 86) electric locomotive No E3141. (Eric Treacy)

left:
An EMU leaves Birmingham New Street with a slow train. (British Railways Board LM Region)

The 08.57 HST from Edinburgh to Kings Cross (via Carlisle) threads its way alongside the river at Wylam in June 1979. (Mrs D A Robinson)

of HSTs had been delivered. Then more high-speed services could be operated, simplifying timetabling, and the 'Scotsman's' schedule was dropped to 4 hours 37 minutes. Further extensions of the use of HSTs came in 1979 when they were introduced on the London–Plymouth route and then to the routes linking Newcastle, Leeds, Manchester, Sheffield and Liverpool with South Wales and the West Country through Birmingham.

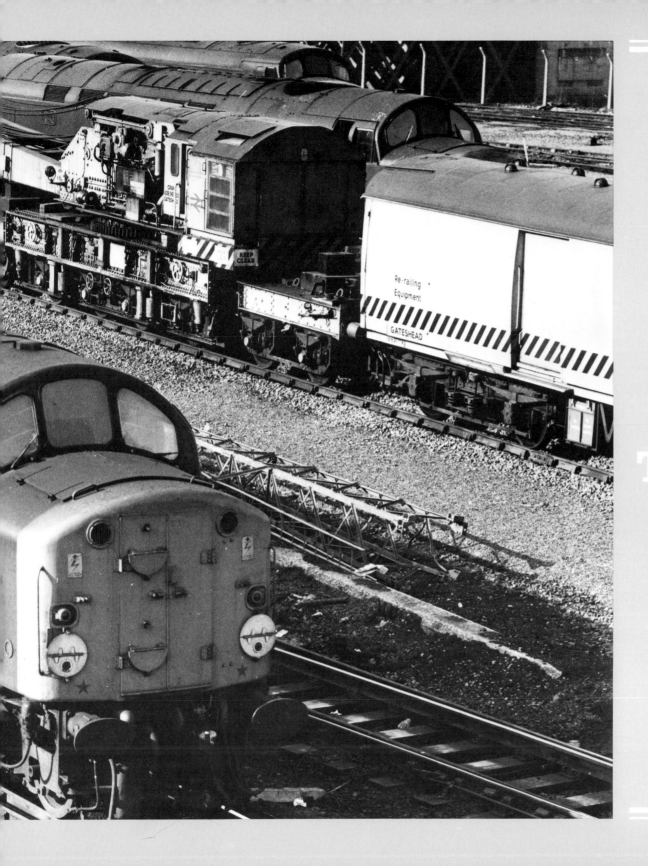

5
TODAY'S RAILWAY

PATTERN FOR THE FUTURE

By the end of the 1970s BR had clearly established methods of operation and hardware on which to build not merely a stable but an expansionary future. However there were considerable causes for concern at the start of the 1980s, and these stemmed from external factors beyond BR's control.

In 1979 BR's passenger business, measured in passenger-mileage, had regained its level of 1961 just before the descent of Beeching's axe. Then the passenger network had been a third larger and family car ownership had been much less common than today. Freight tonnage in 1979 was at the lowest level in British rail history because of the deliberate rejection of so much wagonload and sundries traffic in Beeching's wake. However, financial loss in the freight sector had been eliminated, because the business discarded was inherently loss-making if competitively priced. Also, BR achieved superior economy of trainload opportunities since the mid-60s. The wagon fleet had been cut by 43 per cent since 1975 thanks to the far more productive employment of resources in the new freight system.

Behind this encouraging facade, though, a serious problem was becoming more threatened by the month. The 1955 Modernisation Plan had induced BR to make a huge investment in new equipment over a fairly short period. The huge fleets of new diesel locomotives, diesel railcars, coaches and so on hurried into service between 1955 and the early 1960s would all become obsolete simultaneously. Even in an economic boom their mass renewal was certain to pose a formidable financing problem. In fact, a vast amount of equipment was approaching the end of its useful life at a time of global economic crisis in the aftermath of the oil price explosion.

By the start of the 1980s BR was suffering from reduced Government support for its passenger operation, severe restraint on its borrowing powers and annual investment limit far lower than that of any mainland European railway of comparable size. These pressures were made worse, first by a long-running steel industry strike which greatly reduced BR's tonnage in that sector – and badly affected coal carryings as well – and then by Britain's worse recession since the 1930s. This situation reversed the previous few years' steady

left:
Class 40 No 40073 heads a Tyne Yard to Carlisle freight past Blaydon in June 1977. (Peter J Robinson)

right:
Two class 46 diesel electric locomotives being serviced: June 1979. (Peter J Robinson)

below:
On the West Coast route class 25 No 25142 takes a permanent way train past Low Gill in March 1980. (Peter J Robinson)

growth of new Inter-City traffic. It also reduced BR's already slimmed freight business.

The railway system already existed on far less public money, size for size, than practically all its European mainland neighbours. Government support for railways is universal and in 1980 the only national railway system in the world still able to break even was the South African, which has the advantage of managing the country's ports. The Belgians, French, Germans and the Italians, for instance, were respectively spending the equivalent of 1.46, 0.82, 0.94 and 1.28 per cent of their Gross National Product in support of their railways, while the British figure was only 0.35 per cent. Only in Sweden were the railways obliged to cover as much of their total costs, including capital investment, out of revenue as BR. While the French Railways, had 45 per cent of their annual expenditure met from central or local government funds, BR had only 29 per cent support.

Successive British Governments might claim that they had raised the value of support by 70 per cent since 1974, when yet another of the post-war serial of Transport Acts was passed. This had abandoned individually calculated grants for specific passenger services in favour of a global contract for operation of the passenger business under what was termed the Public Service Obligation (PSO). Since 1974 the PSO grant has been the major source of BR's public money and its value has not kept pace with inflation. The *real* value of BR's financial support has, in fact, slumped by about 20 per cent since 1974.

The real-money value of BR's Government-imposed investment ceiling in 1980 makes an even more depressing comparison against what was being spent under the 1955 Modernisation Plan. Translated into 1980's values, BR's investment in 1960 was worth about £750 millions. At the time of writing BR face the renewal 'bulge' which that outlay stored up for the future with the means and authority to spend little more than £250 millions. This is almost £100 millions short of the minimum needed to keep BR up-to-date as a business concern, supposing there was no renewal 'bulge'. To cope with the obsolescence of so much Modernisation Plan equipment BR needs to invest at least £50 millions a year more; and more still to start a programme of main-line electrification. BR Chairman Sir Peter Parker was warning at the start of 1981 that if BR's investment limit remained at the same real-money level, '3,000 miles of track will be unusable by 1990 simply because we cannot safely and adequately maintain them.'

One Western Region announcement at the start of 1981 fore-shadowed the sad course of events likely to occur on several routes

left:
Class 40 No 40060 takes the new deviation line at Penmanshiel with the 8.10 Glasgow to Scarborough train in August 1980. (Peter J Robinson)

right:
The old LNWR/LMS line from Birmingham to London (Euston) was completely electrified on the 25 Kv system in 1967. Here, in the early days, is one of the hourly e.m.u. sets stopping at most station en route.

below:
The wooden trestle bridge at Barmouth (seen from the south end) on the Cambrian section. (P B Whitehouse)

away from the key trunk lines radiating from London and across country from North-East to North-West or South-West. It was to the effect that from May 1982 through locomotive-hauled trains from Hereford and Worcester to Paddington via Oxford would have to be replaced by diesel multiple-unit connections with other Inter-City services at Oxford. The reason for this was that BR could not afford the £1.5 millions needed to renew the life-expired track of the Cotswold line between Worcester and Oxford. Without that renewal the track could no longer withstand the wear and tear of Class 47 and 50 diesels at 75 to 90mph.

It must be said that BR was forced into taking harsh decisions of this kind. While the Department of Transport strictly controlled major investments in new fleets of locomotives and multiple-units for example, the allocation of PSO money was left to BR, who had to decide which passenger services to develop and which to let fall apart, given an ever-reducing annual PSO grant towards upkeep. BR was statutorily obliged to generate enough passenger revenue to bridge the gap between the PSO grant and ever inflating costs, therefore, it had to concentrate its constricted maintenance funds on

the most heavily-trafficked routes. They could not spend money on relaying a secondary Inter-City route on schedule if those funds were needed to keep, say, the Paddington–Bristol–Cardiff routes fit for maximum Inter-City 125 pace throughout.

The Central Wales line from Swansea to Shrewsbury was barred to locomotives in 1981 because of deferred track renewal, but an infinitely more serious deterioration threatened the Cambrian line. It was suddenly discovered that a breed of sea-worm originating in the Caribbean had been destroying the wooden piles of the Barmouth Bridge. At least £1½ millions would be needed to restore the structure and maintain a rail service to the Cambrian coast – a sum far beyond the resources of BR or of the equally strained budgets of the Welsh authorities. A start costing some £500,000 was made in 1981 allpwing dmus only to cross the structure. The Government suggested that the financial crisis would be at least eased if the railway unions agreed to more rationalisation and job-shedding productivity schemes. This was perfectly true. But union leaders had already cooperated in a reduction of BR staff from over 450,000 pre-Beeching to little more than 170,000. They were unwilling to agree to more job losses unless the Government was prepared to give a firm commitment to allow the substantial investment needed.

An obvious opportunity for reduction of labour costs was the introduction of single-manning for suitable types of train. The need

above:
Barmouth bridge from the north (swing section) in steam days. The building of the railway virtually ended the river traffic and this costly piece of engineering proved to be little used. (P B Whitehouse)

EMU No 313059 comes out of the tunnel into Hadley Wood Station on its way to London, Moorgate, using the up fast line due to engineering works, June 1978. (Peter Howard)

Class 47 No 47027 leaves
Parson's Tunnel between
Exeter and Newton Abbot
with a North to West route
Manchester to Plymouth
express in May 1975.
(Peter J Robinson)

A York Works built three car e.m.u. set for the Great Northern suburban electrification out of Kings Cross. (British Rail)

right:
Bulk haulage of freight in containers (some international) is now a regular feature of operation. Special inland ports such as that in Birmingham have been built to deal with these services. (Colourviews Picture Library)

to carry a guard in the locomotive cab of a modern continuously air-braked freight train no longer exists. To-day's high-performance freight vehicles are safer on the move and automatic devices to detect malfunction, such as hot boxes or dragging equipment are now available. French railwaymen have already accepted single-manning of freight trains with the fallback of two-way driver-ground control radio-telephonic communication. BR has developed its own design of radio link, but just the sight of electric multiple-units equipped to evaluate it in the Kings Cross inner suburban area of Eastern Region was enough to provoke industrial action. Single-manning could be as safe with electric commuter trains as with freight trains, provided that the former were all fitted with sliding doors under the driver's control, which is standard practice on the latest designs of BR multiple-unit. But the investment needed to install the radio communication system is a barrier to early realisation of single-manning on the commuter networks in any event.

The freight sector was urgently in need of a reduction of man-power and the unions had agreed to explore the possibilities in their 1980 wage agreement. BR's efficient traffic in bulk movement between private sidings of coal, ore, oil, chemicals, aggregates was close to its maximum potential market, but in the market for other freight, especially high-rated consumer goods, wagonload traffic was still declining because of uncompetitive service quality and cost. In Freightliners and Speedlink, BR has effective systems of tightly-controlled container trains and air-braked wagonload freight trains with which to compete for the bigger share of this market. The railways must seize this opportunity to keep its Railfreight operation in the black and also to make full use of its main line operating capacity.

Obsolete equipment has to be discarded. Vacuum-braked wagons which had a dismally low productivity because of their time in yards and their 45mph limit; marshalling yards, not excluding those expensively automated; even routes that had lost their relevance all need replacement. Reverence for the old railway maps has to be broken. Increasingly flows of present-day traffic for which rail could compete have come about from a relocation or restructuring of industry that had no geographical relation to the traditional pattern of railway operation. If it is to be won there are many cases where railwaymen must be prepared to demolish old operating 'frontiers' and accept new patterns of through working to avoid arbitrary, un-necessary and expensive crew-changes en route.

Overnight elimination of all vacuum-braked freight working is impossible. It will persist for some years for coal movement to

installations incapable of accepting 51-tonnes capacity, airbraked, Merry-Go-Round type hopper, and for scrap. But for the valuable wagonload business, highly sensitive to transit times, BR must as quickly as possible coax customers to adapt their private sidings, their loading and their discharge arrangements to accept the high-capacity, air-braked wagons to which the expanding Speedlink network is restricted.

The Manchester Division of the LMR at the start of 1981 showed the extent of BR's exclusion from the general merchandise market. Of its total traffic, 92 per cent was moving in trainloads (82 per cent in privately-owned wagons), and all but one per cent was originating in private sidings. Almost 95 per cent of the Division's originating tonnage consisted of limestone, cement and other aggregates ferried chiefly from the quarries of the Peak District to industrial plant and construction railheads in the North-West. This was all highly organised, profitable business, but with hardly any merchandise traffic. The Division was operating three Freightliner terminals, at Trafford Park (for deep-sea trade), Longsight (for domestic traffic) and the Barton Dock Road Containerbase. But it had just two surviving public wagonload depots for the whole area, at Ardwick and Bolton – and one of those was likely to go before long.

In 1981 Manchester was confronted with the first really traumatic consequence of the new Railfreight reshaping drive – the likely closure of the Woodhead route from Sheffield which the LNER had started to electrify at 1500 volts DC before the last war. The hope then was that the line itself would attract very heavy freight tonnage, and that the scheme would also stimulate a spread of electrification. But by the end of the 1970s the route's throughput was down to about 25 trains each way daily; half the level at the start of electric working in 1955 and a third of what the LNER had projected in the late 1930s. The decline was mainly by a shift in National Coal Board sources of supply to the public utilities and industry of the North-West. That had severely cut the tonnages of coal over Woodhead summit from South Yorkshire. Still further losses were in prospect when the great new coalfield near Selby came on stream. Meanwhile no compensating new flows of freight from the Sheffield area occurred.

So, with the Woodhead route's fixed electrification equipment approaching the end of its life, BR conducted intensive traffic surveys. They concluded that the other trans-Pennine routes had the capacity between them to accommodate all the traffic offering and likely to be offered. The case for electrifying them at 25,000 volts AC made more financial sense than re-electrifying the Woodhead line, even though Woodhead (finished in 1955) was the newest of the trans-Pennine routes' tunnels. Complete closure of the Woodhead route

between Penistone and Hadfield was consequently planned from mid 1981. Not long afterwards BR announced that it sought to shut down another once-vital freight route, the Spalding–March line that fed wagonload traffic from the North for East Anglia and the South-East into Whitemoor Yard.

The quest for a more cost-effective railway was not only limited to depressing cut backs, however. BR experimented with a number of promising alternatives which had been designed to replace the existing loss-making equipment in operation on rural lines, on the East Suffolk line in 1981. The probable £$\frac{3}{4}$ million cost of a four-car unit of the Class 210 diesel-electric type BR had designed as a successor to its Modernisation Plan diesel-mechanical multiple-units was too high for many lightly used lines. Few, if any, of the rural routes BR had to finance within the PSO grant could bear the 210's cost. The Research & Development Division came up with a much cheaper alternative. This was the marriage of standard British Leyland single-decker coach body and engine with a high-performance, two-axle

underframe devised for 75mph freight wagons and developed as part of the exhaustive research into vehicle riding which was the research programme leading to the Advanced Passenger Train running gear. The result, known as the Leyland Experimental Vehicle (LEV) and now designated Class 140 in BR's traction fleet, was exhaustively tested and proved smooth-riding and quiet at up to 75mph. It was a great improvement on the railbuses which BR had sampled and soon rejected under the 1955 Modernisation Plan.

As soon as trials had confirmed the LEV's potential, the US Government's Federal Railroad Administration asked to borrow it. Across the Atlantic there was a demand for the revival of rural services in some states. The LEV appeared to be a suitable answer to these demands, provided that it could handle the neglected and ram-shackle condition of the track on the US branches at issue. So the prototype was shipped to New England and performed sufficiently well for the Americans to order a British-built prototype before they returned the original LEV to BR. Back home, meanwhile, the original design was developing into a version capable of formation into multiple-units.

At the same time BR was perfecting a much cheaper means of traffic regulation than orthodox signalling on lighty-used, remote lines such as the Cambrian and the Highland north of Inverness. Essentially it was the historic American despatching method, now refined by the use of simple open-channel radio to give instructions from a central despatcher to drivers and keep a communications link between trains and control continuously open. This basic principle was capable of wide and valuable development. For instance, track-mounted devices could be arranged to actuate junction points and automatically transmit the corresponding advice of route-setting to the drivers' cab instruments upon a radio command from the despatcher's post. The cost of level crossings, still a burden on many rural lines, could be cut by having a radio link over which the despatcher could monitor their safe working and by which motorists communicate with him in an emergency.

Early in 1981 BR selected the 50-mile East Suffolk line from Ipswich to Lowestoft as a proving-ground for a number of experiments. They combined LEV operation (with three two-car units supplemented by a conventional bogie two-car diesel set in the peak), radio signalling and additional single-tracking where the timetable would be two-hourly. They gradually automated the 20 level crossings on the line still worked by signalmen or crossing-keepers, and also experimented with a new kind of two-piece concrete sleeper which would allow age-rotted wooden sleepers to be replaced without the high cost of lifting the rails and their fastenings. If all went well, the line's running costs could equal its annual revenue of £400,000,

Class 47 No 47237 heads a South Wales Merry-Go-Round train (empty stock) en route to Cwmbargoed open cast site in May 1979. (Peter J Robinson)

left & below:
Two scenes at Folkestone
Warren showing Charing
Cross–Ramsgate–Charing
Cross trains on the now
electrified (third rail) system
to the Kent Coast.
(Mrs D A Robinson)

right:
One of the popular Motorail
trains from London
(Kensington) to Carlisle and
Perth in the Lune Gorge
near Tebay in September
1978. (Peter J Robinson)

Electric class 87 No 87013 complete with Mk III coaching stock races through Penrith with an evening Glasgow to Birmingham express in July 1977. (Peter J Robinson)

whereas in 1981 its expenses bled the PSO of an annual £800,000 to balance the account. Many other BR rural services were operating on just as heavy support from the PSO grant, so that the success of the East Suffolk experiment would be very good for BR's finances.

Electronics have made spectacular advances in the past two decades, and they are one assurance of the railways future. Strictly-disciplined operation on fixed tracks makes the railway the only transport medium capable of maximising the 'micro-chip revolution's' potential for high-speed decision-making and automated control. BR can bring complicated route systems and intensive traffic under the command of one signalling centre, because of a tiny micro-chip's ability to transmit and receive as many as 500 bits of information per second. One of BR's most ambitious electronic signalling schemes yet is under way at the London end of the SR's South Eastern and Central divisions. On its completion in 1983 the nerve centre of this project at Clapham Junction will govern 267 track-miles extending from Victoria and Holborn Viaduct down the Brighton and Kent Coast main lines to Thornton Heath, Sutton and Sevenoaks. It will control 75 stations and almost 1,350 trains loaded with more than 220,000 passengers daily. Until the start of the scheme the area it covers needs the control of 35 different pre-electronic signalboxes.

The application of electronic controls systems to electric traction units, eliminates mechanisms prone to wear and reduces maintenance costs to a much lower level than those of diesel locomotives. This adds more weight to the case for the resumption of BR main-line electrification. In spite of Britain's North Sea oil reserves mounting evidence shows the superior economy of electrical operation on busy trunk routes. In real money terms, too, technical development is lowering the deterrent first cost of electrification.

Since completion of the West Coast electrification to Glasgow, BR has been restricted to suburban projects. The installation of 25,000 volts AC Eastern Region's Kings Cross inner and outer suburban area and then on neighbouring LMR Midland line from Bedford to St. Pancras and Moorgate, has been a notable example. One or two modest infills of operationally irritating gaps in existing 25,000 volt AC territory also took place. In the spring of 1978, the Government set up a joint BR-Department of Transport study group to 'review the case for a programme of main-line electrification, to analyse the relevant considerations and formulate the issues for decision.'

Published early in 1981, the group's searching analysis of all possible technological and economic scenarios not only made an unassailable financial case for electrification, but for electrification on the widest practicable scale as quickly as possible. Reduced energy costs, the

right:
The West Coast 25kV main line at Low Gill, Westmorland with class 83 No 83009 heading a Crewe to Glasgow parcels train in March 1980. (Peter J Robinson)

ability to work traffic with smaller traction fleets because of electric units' reliability and the halving of maintenance bills were significant factors in favour of electrification. Passenger train crew costs could be reduced by 10 per cent and those of freight trains by 20 per cent. The financial return on the investment in the biggest network conversion proposal was a healthy 11 per cent – more if it could be executed in 20 rather than 30 years.

The biggest of the network electrification options considered covered 5,750 route-miles, just over half BR's system, and would put 83 per cent of all BR passenger traffic and 68 per cent of its freight under the wires. At the 1978 price levels cited in the report this scheme would require an addition to BR investments of £576 million over the 20-year period. The cost of the fixed electrification works would actually be almost £150 million more, but that extra would be offset by the lower cost of new electric as opposed to diesel-powered rolling stock. If the Government accepted the need to renew all the 1955 Modernisation Plan diesel equipment and set that expense against the electrification budget, then the electrification would demand no more than an extra £30 million a year – and that for an infinitely more reliable and competitive rail service.

A Midlands to North East express – the 07.30 Birmingham to York and Newcastle train nears Durham in March 1978.

When the report emerged BR was waiting for Government approval to extend its Eastern Region electrification from Royston and Bishops Stortford to Cambridge, and from Colchester to Ipswich, Harwich and Norwich on a timetable projecting completion in 1988. If the Government accepted the report's findings and authorised one of its bigger network options, BR expected to have the first main-line conversion well under way by 1983.

First electrification to be completed would be that from Hitchin to Leeds and Bradford, because the East Coast main routes had already been rationalised and resignalled in anticipation of this happening, however, the London Midland Region main line from St. Pancras to the East Midlands and Sheffield, considered the priority candidate for conversion, had not. The Midland would be next for completion. The order of precedence after these, put the East Coast main line from Doncaster to Edinburgh first, the Western Region from Paddington to Bristol and South Wales, followed by the Plymouth main line, the North-East/South-West artery throughout and a Trans-Pennine route. This was apart from extending 25,000 volt connections from the West Coast main line to Liverpool and Manchester (for Scottish traffic) and Blackpool.

In 1981 BR was also hoping for a happy ending to the long-running Channel Tunnel serial. At the end of 1974 the Labour Government had cancelled an Anglo-French agreement to build a double-track tunnel with sufficient clearance to operate an outsize road-vehicle rail ferry shuttle. By 1979 BR and French Railways had worked up a new economy-size design for a single-bore, confined to orthodox passenger and freight trains, and without the financially controversial high-speed railway from the Channel coast to London which was part of the earlier plan. Trains were to move through the tunnel in convoys alternating by direction, each convoy occupying the tunnel for one hour of the 18 daily it would be open to traffic. The planners reckoned that this would allow a throughput of 60 trains each way daily if speed were limited to 75mph, or daily 90 if it were thought worth investing for 100mph. Traction would be 25,000 Volts AC, requiring a fleet of dual-voltage locomotives to work trains through from London over the SR's third rail DC system to the French coastline. The Government promised to pronounce a decision in principle before 1981 was out.

right:
A 4 car d.m.u. leaves Hull, Paragon, station with a train for Leeds in January 1981. (Peter J Robinson)

INTER CITY, HST AND APT

The 11.00 Glasgow to Euston train, complete with Mk III stock takes the Midland route over Ais Gill in January 1977. (Mrs D A Robinson)

The HSTs made a spectacular debut on the 'Inter-City 125' services from Paddington to Bristol and South Wales and from Kings Cross to the North and Scotland in the late 1970s, but the 1980s opened with a frustrating lull in further development, either of speed or of other service qualities. The reasons were uncertainty over electrification and over perfection of the APT, compounded by the government limits on BR expenditure.

The APT had been developed for 25,000 volt AC electric traction in the 1970s. Its benefit to the unelectrified Paddington–Bristol/South Wales and East Coast main lines would be comparatively small. Both routes had either been built with sufficient freedom from curvature or had had the worst of their speed-limiting features 'ironed out', which allowed them to make the most of the conventionally suspended HST's 125mph capability. That was not so on the Electrified West Coast main line from Euston, which has as well as curves, severe gradients north of Lancaster where the high power/weight ratio of the aerodynamic APT would be valuable. Speed levels on this route had been virtually static since 1974 and a fresh advance was necessary to counter-attack the thriving London–Glasgow air shuttle and a similar threat between London and Manchester.

Three prototype APT sets designated APT-P were to have carried their first fare-paying passengers in 1979. In each set two 4,000hp power cars were sandwiched between two sections of six passenger cars, an operational layout which demanded separate catering provision in each section, but which was enforced by the desirability on technical grounds of having the two power cars together. However, the full 8,000hp of two power cars was needed only if the APTs were to run regularly at 150mph. This was unlikely to happen for some time because it would be unacceptable without the costly installation of a continuous cab signalling system throughout each APT route. It would also be impracticable without increasing the capacity of the traction current supply system to absorb the power demands of several APTs simultaneously working at top speed. It was decided, therefore, that the concept would be revised as the APT-S for series production. This was a push-pull unit with a single end power car and

The 08.00 London (Kings Cross) to Edinburgh HST (254001) nears Houndwood in September 1979. (Peter J Robinson)

11 trailers which would be powerful enough for 125mph operation.

The reduction of journey times possible even at this lower maximum was considerable because of the APT's quicker negotiation of curves. The draft schedule for the APT-P, restricted in public service to 125mph, envisaged a London–Glasgow journey time of $4\frac{1}{2}$hr with two intermediate stops which was 45min less than the fastest previously scheduled for an orthodox locomotive-hauled train. A quicker time still might be possible when the whole service was APT-equipped and the planners no longer had the difficult job of pathing one or two APTs, with their superior curving speed and 125mph maximum, through a timetable otherwise full of conventional 100mph Inter-City trains.

Inauguration has been repeatedly deferred although private demonstration runs confirm all the tilt-body suspension's promise of banking the cars through curves up to 40 per cent faster than usual. When this happens the passengers would scarcely notice the abnormality unless they glanced up and noticed one horizon sinking below the window frames. (The rapid change of floor angle through a reverse curve, though, is disconcerting to anyone standing up, and BR realise that they would have to reduce speed through a few such bends if APTs were to feature a full meal service.) Different items of the mass of new technology packed into the APT have, unfortunately, shown up failures which have prevented BR from embarking on public service until they have been eradicated. The Government is not prepared to endorse APT-S construction until the three APT-Ps have had a year's track record of reliable public service.

The Heaton traction and coaching stock depot at Newcastle upon Tyne showing an Inter-City 125 train undergoing maintenance. (British Rail)

GENERAL ARRANGEMENT OF POWER CAR.

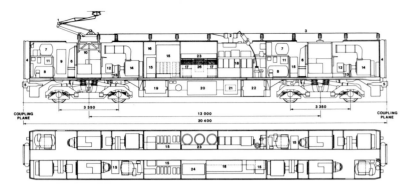

1 PANTOGRAPH.
2 CIRCUIT BREAKER.
3 H.T. BUS-BAR.
4 GANGWAY CONNECTION.
5 DRAWBAR.
6 HYDROKINETIC BRAKE RADIATOR & FAN.
7 HYDROKINETIC BRAKE AIR RESERVOIR.
8 HYDROKINETIC BRAKE WATER RESERVOIR.
9 DOOR.
10 PANTOGRAPH ANTI-TILT MECHANISM.

11 HYDROKINETIC BRAKE CONTROLS.
12 HYDROKINETIC BRAKE.
13 TRANSMISSION GEARBOX.
14 TRACTION MOTOR & BLOWER.
15 ELECTRIC CONTROL EQUIPMENT.
16 AIR COMPRESSOR.
17 COOLING FAN FOR TRANSFORMER,CHOKE, THYRISTOR & TILT SYSTEMS.
18 THYRISTOR CONVERTORS.
19 CHOKE.

20 RADIATORS FOR TRANSFORMER,CHOKE, THYRISTORS & TILT SYSTEMS.
21 THYRISTOR COOLANT TANK & PUMP.
22 TRANSFORMER.
23 BATTERIES.
24 TILT SYSTEM CONTROL PACK.
25 FIRE EXTINGUISHER GAS BOTTLES.
26 VENTILATION FAN.

Meanwhile the diesel HST output is coming to an end at 95 sets, instead of almost double that number as projected in the mid-1970s. One reason is the growing confidence that more main-line electrification will be approved and the APT-S in mass production soon. Another was the Government's obvious scepticism that the cost of 125mph equipment was justified unless the top speed could be used. The HSTs' limitation by curvature and signalling to 90mph over all but 36 miles of the Paddington to Plymouth line make their introduction to Plymouth look unjustified, even though their employment cut the best total overall journey time to a record $3\frac{1}{4}$hr. It will be some time before resignalling and curve realignment allow even 110mph on a few stretches of this line west of Reading.

Thus by 1981 BR's diesel locomotives are obsolescent and, with the likely date for availability of the first squadron of APT-Ps now as far ahead as 1985, there is a possibility that the HST production line might have to be revived, if not for more diesel-powered sets then for

far left:
A drawing showing the general arrangement of the power car on the APT. (British Rail)

left:
Rocket 150 Cavalcade Participant. The Advanced Passenger Train – Prototype (APT – P) – one of the three 125mph units being used for service evaluation between London and Glasgow waits to join the Rainhill Parade. The train comprises two 4000hp electric power cars and twelve passenger coaches. (British Rail)

right:
A 1981 advertisement put out by British Railways to promote the new image of the APT/HST. (G F Allen collection)

How to keep going during the next energy crisis.

It might seem that with North Sea oil, the energy crisis is behind us.

In fact, it's in front of us.

About twenty years away at best, calculate the experts.

Then wells everywhere in the world, including our own, will start to run dry.

The 1977 report of the Workshop on Alternative Energy Strategies, sponsored by the Massachusetts Institute of Technology, concluded that "the supply of oil will fail to meet increasing demand before the year 2000, most probably between 1985 and 1995".

A recent Government paper, by the Advisory Council on Energy Conservation, came to much the same conclusion.

So Britain has got to develop a transport system that doesn't depend on oil.

Which is one important reason for continuing to electrify our railways.

Electric trains will run on any source of energy: coal, nuclear, gas or oil.

Railway electrification now means we can keep going in the future.

British Rail
The backbone of the nation.

an electric version to upgrade the west Coast main line to 'Inter-City 125' status before mid-1985. In face of air competition BR cannot leave speed standards between London and North-West England and Scotland where they are any longer.

Several schemes to make the use of rail more convenient and attractive to passengers for local travel in the provincial conurbations took place in the late 1970s. Among the reasons for this was the need to safeguard the environment by discouraging private cars and their parking lots. On Merseyside a new underground loop and link line beneath the centre of Liverpool knitted together the Southport, Ormskirk, West Kirby, Rock Ferry and Garston electric lines of the Merseyrail system operated by BR for the Merseyside Public Transport Executive. Through running between Southport and Garston on the system's Northern line via the new link and circular operation of

the Wirral lines' trains over the new subterranean loop eliminated the costly train turnrounds in the city centre of the old network. It also created easy interchange between Northern and Wirral lines' services at a new subterranean Moorfields station and brought trains from both routes to stations much more convenient for city-centre access. The operational simplicity of the revised network allowed a substantial increase in peak-hour frequency of service. This development, with the support of measures to encourage the extension of suburban station parking space and the first steps in getting suburban bus services to act as feeders of well laid-out bus-rail interchanges, has stimulated a 30 per cent increase in passenger carrying.

Together, with this development, the Liverpool–Southport line received BR's latest commuter electric multiple-units. These have centrally-operated sliding doors, inter-car communication, public address, new smooth-riding bogies with secondary air suspension and dynamically-operated disc brakes, and an acceleration rate of 0.72m/sec to a top speed of 75mph. The type first appeared as the Class 313 for the Eastern Region's Kings Cross suburban network.

The power unit is dual-voltage 25,000 volt AC/750 volt DC, the DC capability for working through the tunnels to Moorgate where third-rail current collection had to be employed for lack of clearance to instal high-voltage overhead wires. The Liverpool–Southport version is the third-rail DC-only Class 507. Class 314 and 315 are AC

A Midland main line 8 car d.m.u. forming a St Pancras to Luton train leaving St Pancras in May 1979. (Peter J Robinson)

Close up of one of the new e.m.u. sets in use on the Tyne and Wear PTE service. (Courtesy G F Allen)

below:
A Tyne & Wear metro set at Haymarket (Newcastle) with a Tynemouth (first line open) and Monkseaton (converted BR section) train. October 1980. (Peter J Robinson)

variations for the Glasgow and ER Liverpool Street inner suburban systems respectively. Class 508 is another third-rail DC type, with which the renewal of the Southern Region's aged fleet of commuter multiple-units was begun in 1980. Before the SR replacement programme had gone very far, however, BR decided for economy's sake to switch to a new design adopting the body-shell of the 75ft-long Inter-City MkIII coach. The Class 508s, therefore, will eventually be transferred to the Wirral to join their Class 507 cousins on the Merseyrail network. The next deliveries for the Southern Region, designated Class 510, and also the four-car 25,000 volt AC Class 317 units for the London–Midland Region's Bedford–St. Pancras/Moorgate electrification would be patterned on the Inter-City MkIII coach body.

The Class 314 stock mentioned above was provided for another important inner-city link-up, the complete rehabilitation of an abandoned tunnel route beneath Glasgow as a modern 25,000 volt AC connection between the city's north (ex-LNER) and south (ex-LMS) 'Blue Train' electric systems. Over this $4\frac{1}{2}$-mile Argyle Line trains can now run straight through the city from Hamilton and

Lanark south of the Clyde to Helensburgh and Balloch in the north. Long-cherished hope of integrating the local railways of Manchester by a tunnel between that city's two termini, the so-called 'Picc-Vic' project, have sadly foundered on cost; but a cheaper alternative, the construction of a connection known as the Castlefield Curve on the surface some way from the city centre, seems to have a fair chance of achievement.

A very different kind of conurbation railway opened its doors for business on Tyneside in 1980. Light Rail Transit (LRT), a very sophisticated development of the urban tramway, has been adopted by many Continental European cities, and more recently by a number of North American cities, as a cheaper, sensible alternative to a full-scale Metro.

The local authority, accepted that Tyneside needed local railways, but was convinced that the orthodox BR lines, with their widely-spaced suburban stations, and remoteness from Newcastle's centre at the city's Central station and costly fixed expenses of traditional signalling and working method, did not meet either financial or convenience criteria. They therefore decided to adapt the suburban lines and extend them beneath central Newcastle as an LRT system. The resulting $33\frac{1}{2}$-mile network (absorbing 26 miles of BR route) will have as many as 41 stations and be operated by economical, light-weight trains with the maximum of simplicity and labour-saving automation.

The inaugural 12-mile Haymarket–Tynemouth section of the so-called Tyne Metro was commissioned in August 1980. Its two-car Metro-Cammell train sets, have a 50mph maximum speed and seat 84 with standing room for 125 more. Stations are unmanned, with automatic ticket-operated turnstiles, and are supervised from a central control by closed-circuit TV. Signalling is basic and the trains, even when full service operates at $2\frac{1}{2}$-minutes frequency in the downtown Newcastle area, set up their own routes and announce themselves automatically at stations. Each driver sets up his own train description and route on cab controls before starting and the data is absorbed by an underfloor electronic device called a transponder. This is automatically interrogated at key points en route by trackside apparatus which not only activates the junction points as required, but also reports the train's progress to the control centre's illuminated diagram and operates the platform train description displays at stations ahead.

The Tyne Metro, hopefully, is a model which other British cities such as Birmingham, Sheffield and the West Riding conurbations will have the resources and imagination to copy in the future.

THE NEW LOOK FREIGHT TRAIN

Three conspicuous changes in the look of British freight trains have taken place since the early 1970s. One is the increasing size of the wagons; another is the increasing proportion of them carrying the names of private owners; and the third is the rising speed of many freight trains. The 45-wagon coal train grossing more than 2,000 tonnes and making 60mph behind a growling, 3,250hp Class 56 diesel is now a commonplace sight on some trunk routes.

The speed results from the steady replacement of the typical short-wheelbase, vacuum-braked wagons of the 1950s with air-braked vehicles designed to a high-performance specification which in many cases makes them capable of 75mph. Air-braking is standard, for example, on the 10,000 51-tonnes gross hopper wagons that now dominate BR's coal movement. BR's squeezed finances had not managed to replace the last of the purely hand-braked freight wagons in use in 1981, but the Southern Region at least was already operating nothing but continuously-braked freight trains anywhere in its territory, though in some cases they were still vacuum-braked. In 1981 40,000 of the 150,000 wagons at work on BR were air-braked.

Increased private ownership of wagons was a tribute to BR's train-load operating methods. Major clients accepted that BR lacked the resources to custom-build wagons for individual traffics. Oil, stone, cement and chemical firms in particular, were convinced of the economy and pipeline reliability of door-to-door bulk movement in trainloads and they were prepared to invest their own money, not only in setting up rail-suited loading and discharge apparatus but also in acquiring or leasing their own special-purpose wagons. The trend was encouraged by the availability under Section 8 of the 1974 Transport Act of 50 per cent Government grants towards the cost of private siding railheads and wagons, provided the use of rail was both cost-saving and environmentally beneficial. By 1981 20,000 privately-owned wagons were in use on BR.

The growing bulk of wagons comes from the ability of modern, deep-ballasted concrete prepared track to accept considerably heavier axle-loads, so that two-axle wagons of up to 50 tons' and bogie vehicles of 100 tons' fully laden weight have become tolerable.

DANGER
IT IS
STRICTLY FORBIDDEN
TO CLIMB ON TOP OF THIS
WAGON WHILST IN THE VICINITY OF
OVERHEAD
ELECTRIC WIRE

far left:
The new private owner
wagon: a train of hoppers
for the Foster Yeoman stone
traffic. (British Rail)

left:
Class 31 No 31324 heading a
train of fitted empties is
overtaken by Class 45
No 45036 heading the
evening Tyneside CFD to
Bescot Speedlink service near
Chester-le-Street in August
1980. (Peter J Robinson)

Class 31 locomotives
Nos 31130 and 31278 head a
loaded potash train from
Bowlby mine in April
1977. (Peter J Robinson)

Latter-day technology has erased almost all the distinction between two-axle and bogie wagons where stability and speed capability are concerned, but maintenance costs favour the two-axle type, besides which, many private sidings are uncomfortable with the length of bogie wagon.

The economic advantage of bigger payload space per vehicle is obvious. Area capacity is especially important in the merchandise freight business not only to compete with road juggernauts but also for ease of loading and unloading palletised goods. Continental wagon-leasing firms such as Cargowaggon and Danzas have probed the limits of the BR loading gauge in the huge 65ft-long bogie vans that are contributing valuably to BR's expanding Continental European freight traffic via the cross-Channel train ferries. The latest of these vans have sliding-door walls that can open up half the bodyside for ease of fork-lift truck loading.

Privately-owned wagons such as these, which conform to BR's high-performance, air-braked wagon specification, are as welcome as BR's own vehicles in Speedlink, the new-generation wagonload

freight service. Speedlink is limited to vehicles of this character. It also differs from the old-style wagonload freight service in that it is not an all-purpose service. The Speedlink network is confined to the big industrial towns and cities and the ports, where there is a chance of obtaining full trainloads or at worst substantial train sections for a common destination. That way Speedlink trains do not need marshalling yards. Many of them run intact as fast trainloads the whole way. Others pause only to exchange ready-assembled sections at key junctions like Warrington, which is the focus of tightly-timed Speedlink interchanges in the North West. As a result overnight reliability can be guaranteed and costly modern wagons get far more productive work under load, because they do not waste hours waiting in yards to be shunted between trains. Every Speedlink consignment is continuously under the electronic eye of TOPS, BR's computerised all-line data processing and traffic control apparatus.

The rail merchandise freight success of the 1970s was Freightliner,

Class 40 No 40165 banked by two class 20s leaves the loop at Beattock with a Winsford (Cheshire) to Millerhill block salt train in August 1979. This is an unusual route for this train but it has been diverted due to the collapse of Penmanshiel tunnel on the East Coast line. (Peter J Robinson)

not in the domestic market where it was hard put to hold its own, but in the inland movement of shipborne export/import containers. In this deepsea traffic it had won the transport of four out of every ten containers entering the country by sea. It became the world's largest single inland haulier of containers, and, despite the recession, its business in this sector was still climbing in the 1980s. A measure of its achievement is that at Southampton the two Freightliner terminals, Maritime and Millbrook, now deal in more tonnage than the dock railway system did in the post-war heyday of conventional rail freight working. The 74 miles of track was then processing an annual average of 3,000 goods trains and 120,000 wagons. With the latest Class 56 freight diesels, operation of Freightliner trains aggregating as many as 25 flatcars, instead of the customary 15 or 20, has become possible provided that the Freightliner terminals concerned can handle the extra train length.

The Merry-Go-Round (MGR) concept of feeding coal-fired

Class 37 No 37055 passes Tyne yard with two empty molten steel carriers. During the summer of 1976 two such trains were being worked daily from the British Steel Corporation Hartlepool to Consett (now closed) during the relining of furnaces at Consett. (Peter J Robinson)

A Merry-Go-Round coal train from Cwmbargoed open cast site descending the bank near Taff Merthyr in May 1979. (Peter J Robinson)

right:
Double headed class 37 locomotives Nos 37007 and 37048 with South Hetton to Blythe coal hoppers near Newcastle, July 1980. (Peter J Robinson)

electricity generating stations with fixed train-sets of air-braked, 32 tons' capacity automatic-discharge hoppers in continuous circuit was further refined in the 1970s. If the big baseload power stations always took their coal from the same collieries MGR would be a perfect re-production of a toy railway's simplicity. Trains would continuously trace the same circuit, running non-stop around power station circular track bisected by discharge hoppers. The wagons would automatically discharge their contents in sequence as their bottom doors are activated by lineside devices while the train speed is held at an unvarying 0.5mph by a special low-speed control.

But the coal movement does not follow a straightforward pattern. Each power station's feed has to be scientifically mixed with different grades of coal for maximum efficiency. Chiefly for this reason a single power station can draw coal from up to 50 different collieries. Central Electricity Generating Board cannot accurately advise BR which collieries will supply which power station until the Thursday before each week's MGR working. This leaves precious little time to draft an MGR timetable of maximum efficiency for the following week, or to advise all staff concerned of its detail before the start of the week's work. The solution to this problem is made possible by the micro-

chip. Each week MGR trains, their locomotives and their crews shift over 300,000 tons of coal from a permutation of some 30 South Yorkshire pitheads to the three huge Aire Valley Power stations – Ferrybridge, Eggborough and Drax. Since the mid-1970s the complex routing and timetabling has been fully worked out in no more than three hours by computers. The computer checks its memory bank to take full account of every possible obstacle to simple work programming, from layout capacities at pitheads and colliery and signalbox opening hours to the times trainmen must be given a break during their shift. The outcome, which covers the weekly running of some 300 trains by 13 Knottingley depot locomotives and 45 train-crews, makes such efficient use of BR resources that these MGR trains are 50 per cent cheaper to run than conventional coal trains. The intensity of the working is such that Drax alone can have as many as 33 trains trundling one after another round its track circle, unloading 1,000 tons of coal or more each, then heading straight back to the coalfield. Within 24 hours one locomotive and train-set can tot up as many as seven circuits from pits to power station and back again.

With the aid of its TOPS computers BR was extending this concept to two-thirds of its entire MGR coal operation in 1981. That would involve planning each week's work for 450 train-crews from traction depots involved in the pipeline flows of coal from 93 collieries to a total of 10 power stations.

58 001

Other commodities beside coal can benefit from the MGR method. One is ore, nowadays imported and needing bulk movement from ore ports to steel plants in a steady, high-volume flow. These are the heaviest trains currently run on BR. Rakes of 100-tons gross wagons, each hauled by a pair of Class 56 diesels, shift over 2,300 tons of ore at a time. These massive trains have to move smartly, too, because they share the South Wales main with BR's 'Inter-City 125s'.

The wagons are known as tipplers. They have special rotatable couplings so that as the train is moved slowly through the discharge plant at the colliery, each wagon in succession can be rotated bodily through 160 degrees to dispose of its contents without the need to detach it from its neighbours. Thus the train is kept intact so that within only 45 minutes of starting to unload it can be emptied and ready to return to Port Talbot.

This is just one impressive example of the advances in technique and technology that have redeveloped the railway as a highly competitive form of transport in the last quarter of the 20th Century. Added to that distinction it has an unquestioned ability to move passengers and freight in bulk at infinitely less cost to the environment than any other overland mode, and – electrified – it promises a transport system that can be made immune to exhaustion of oil supplies. The first 150 years were, hopefully, no more than an overture to a still more exciting future.

Although there were many narrow-gauge railway systems extant in England and Wales and one in Scotland, few of these fell into the hands of the main-line companies. The LMS inherited the Leek & Manifold in Derbyshire; the Southern took the Lynton & Barnstaple in Devon; the Great Western took the Welshpool & Llanfair, the Corris and the Vale of Rheidol in Wales. The latter still runs as a tourist line and is British Railways' only steam-operated section.
(P B Whitehouse)

INDEX